EAST A

TEASHOP
WALKS

Jean Patefield

COUNTRYSIDE BOOKS
NEWBURY BERKSHIRE

Cover illustration by Colin Doggett
Photographs and maps by the author

Produced through The Letterworks Ltd., Reading
Typeset by CJWT Solutions, St Helens
Printed by Berforts Information Press, Oxford

Contents

Walk

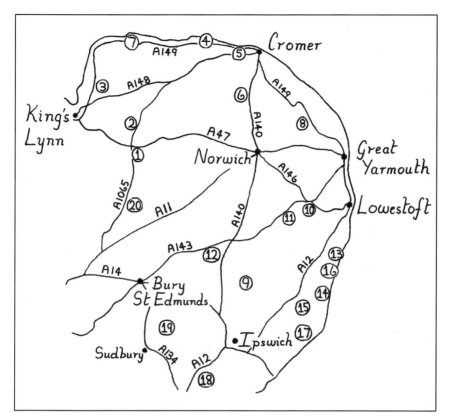

Area map showing the locations of the walks.

KEY TO SKETCH MAPS

Path on route	– – →	Sea	~ ~ ~	Point in text	⑥
Path not on route	•••	Church	†	Car park	▭
Road	===	Teashop	☕	Building referred to in text	■
River	∿∿∿	Pub referred to in text	PH		

Introduction

What exactly is East Anglia? Norfolk and Suffolk have always been at its core but there are as many different definitions as there are authorities, many (but not all) including Essex and Cambridgeshire but also extending out to Lincolnshire, Bedfordshire and even as far as Hertfordshire. It is a historical rather than a geographic unit. When the Romans retreated from their Empire the Angles came from what is now Denmark and established the Kingdom of East Anglia in the 6th century. Before King Egbert united England in a single kingdom in AD 829, East Anglia consisted only of Suffolk and Norfolk; Essex, the land of the East Saxons, was not included. I have taken as my boundary that ancient kingdom.

The image of East Anglia is not one of stimulating scenery, captured in Noel Coward's immortal line, 'Very flat, Norfolk'. It is true there are no dramatic valleys, no towering peaks. This is a gentle and unassuming landscape which does not impose itself on the visitor but whose charms wait to be sought out. There is immense variety here - ancient heaths, rivers and broads, wide marshes, crumbling cliffs and a gently rolling, pastoral countryside which has evolved over centuries. There have been great changes as agriculture has been mechanised but there are still many very attractive parts. One of the most appealing aspects of exploring East Anglia is the interesting and historic towns and villages, many of which have excellent teashops.

The 20 walks described in this book aim to give a taste of all the landscapes to be enjoyed. They are all between 3 and 6½ miles and should be well within the capacity of the average person, including those of mature years and families with children. They are intended to take the walker through this attractive corner of England at a gentle pace with plenty of time to stop and stare, to savour the beauty and interest all around. To fully appreciate the countryside it is necessary to go slowly with your eyes and ears open.

All the routes are on public rights of way or permissive paths and have been carefully checked but, of course, in the countryside things do change; a gate is replaced by a stile or a wood is extended. Each walk is circular and is illustrated by a sketch map. An Ordnance Survey map is useful as well, especially for identifying the main features of views. The area is covered by Explorer 1:25 000 series sheets 196, 197, 211, 212, 229, 230, 231, 236, 238, 250, 251, 252 and OL40. The grid reference of the starting point and the number of the appropriate Explorer map are given for each walk.

The walks are designed so that, starting where suggested, the teashop is reached in the second half so a really good appetite for tea can be worked up and then its effects walked off. Some walks start at a car park, which is ideal. Where this is not possible, the recommended starting place will always have somewhere where a few cars can be left without endangering other traffic. However, it sometimes fits in better with the plans for the day to start and finish at the teashop and so for each walk there are details of how to do this.

Tea is often said to be the best meal to eat out in England and I believe that it is something to be enjoyed on all possible occasions. Scones with cream and strawberry jam, delicious home-made cakes, toasted teacakes dripping with butter in winter, delicate cucumber sandwiches in summer, all washed down with the cup that cheers! Bad for the figure maybe, but the walking will see to that.

The best teashops serve a range of cakes, all home-made and including fruit cake as well as scones and other temptations. They always have at least light lunches available as well so there is no need to think of these walks as just something for the afternoons.

The pleasures of summer walking are obvious. However, let me urge you not to overlook the pleasures of a good walk in winter. The roads and paths are quieter and what could be better than sitting by an open fire in a cosy teashop scoffing crumpets that you can enjoy with a clear conscience due to the brisk walk to get them!

Teashops are not scattered evenly through East Anglia. In some places popular with tourists, the visitor is spoilt for choice. In such cases the teashop that, in the author's opinion, most closely fulfils the criteria set out above is recommended but, should that not appeal, there are others from which to choose. In other places where there is a delightful walk to be enjoyed the choice is more limited. However, they all offer a good tea partway round an attractive walk. The opening times and telephone number of each teashop is given. Some are rather vague about when they open out of season - it seems to depend on weather and mood. If you are planning a walk on a wet November Tuesday, for example, a call to check that tea will actually be available that day is a wise precaution. A few are definitely closed in the depths of winter and for these walks an alternative source of refreshment is given. In most cases, these are pubs serving food which sometimes includes tea.

So put on your walking shoes and prepare to be delighted, by the East Anglian scenery and a traditional English tea!

Jean Patefield

Walk 1
SWAFFHAM

The focus of this walk is Swaffham, sometimes considered the finest Regency town in Norfolk. The community really comes to life on Saturday when it is very lively with a bustling market. The route is on well-made paths and lanes and is very easy to follow. It makes use of sections of the long distance path, the Peddars Way, and a path along an old railway line. This part of north-west Norfolk has pleasant rolling countryside with productive farmland well supplied with trees and attractive views.

 The Tea Pot in Plowright Place, Swaffham, is ideally positioned just off the Market Square and has some tables outside in summer in the attractive courtyard. It is very popular with locals visiting the market. True to its name, it is decorated with, at the last count, some 192 teapots. A good selection of cakes is offered as well as tasty toasted pannini with fillings such as brie and bacon or roasted vegetables with mozzarella cheese, supplemented if you wish with delicious soup. The Tea Pot is open between 9 am and 4 pm every day throughout the year except Sundays. Telephone: 01760 722301.

When the teashop is closed there are several pubs in Swaffham which serve food, notably the Red Lion on the opposite side of Market Square. In addition, food is available at the service area by the roundabout near the start of the walk.

DISTANCE: 5 miles.

MAP: OS Explorer 236 King's Lynn, Downham Market & Swaffham.

STARTING POINT: The junction of the A47 Norwich-King's Lynn road and the Peddars Way near Swaffham (GR 843094).

HOW TO GET THERE: At a roundabout with services on the A47, 1½ miles east of its junction with the A1065, turn south towards Swaffham. After 50 yards take a road on the left, signed as a no through road. This is the old road and there are several spots where a car can be left without causing inconvenience.

ALTERNATIVE STARTING POINT: If you want to visit the teashop at the beginning or end of your walk, start in Swaffham. On any day except Saturday, parking is allowed in the Market Square, which somewhat detracts from its gracious appearance. There is a long stay car park on Theatre Street and this is signed from the Market Square. Walk back to the Market Square and the teashop is to the left in Plowright Place. You will then start the walk at point 6.

THE WALK

1. Walk to the closed off end of the road and turn right along the Peddars Way for about 600 yards.

The Peddars Way is a long distance footpath which runs from Knettishall, just in Suffolk, to Holme-next-the-Sea. It follows the line of a Roman road built soon after AD 61, following the revolt of the Iceni and Trinovantes led by Boadicea, to enable troops to be moved to police the area. What exists today is not at all complete. Many stretches were originally built on an embankment of whatever material was available locally and then topped with gravel to make a road bed sometimes 2 ft 6 inches thick. As is usual with Roman roads, built for an army that depended on its feet, it is very straight. Quite why it should finish at the sea is not known. One plausible suggestion is that there was a ferry port at Holme connecting Norfolk with Lincolnshire across the Wash. The name Peddars Way is not of Roman origin. It first appears on a map of 1587 and probably means simply footpath, from the Latin pedester, to go on foot.

2. Turn right along a broad crosstrack. Follow this, ignoring a track on the left and keeping ahead when the main track turns right until

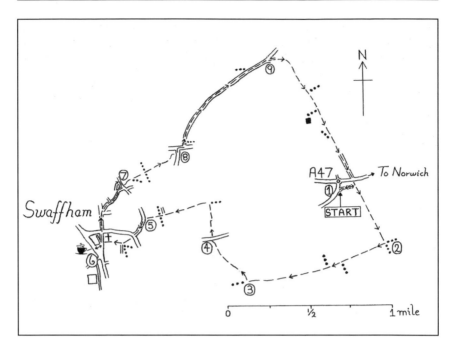

it crosses a disused railway line and then continue for a further 300 yards.

3. Turn right on a waymarked, hedged path to a road.

4. Turn right then left almost immediately on a public footpath, signed 'Sporle Road ¾'. At a T-junction with a crosspath turn left and follow the path to a T-junction with a road.

5. Turn left and walk to a further T-junction. Take a public footpath directly opposite. Follow the path past the end of a road called Campinglands and through the churchyard. Bear left across Market Square to Plowright Place and the teashop.

All over Norfolk there are attractive carved town and village signs depicting some aspect of local history. Edward VII originated the idea, erecting signs on the villages of the Sandringham estate to encourage local people to take an interest in the history of their neighbourhood. The practice caught on and Swaffham's sign was one of the first, erected in 1929. It was carved by Harry Carter, nephew of the archaeologist Howard Carter who discovered Tutankhamun's tomb. It shows John

Chapman, also known as The Peddlar. The story goes that he had a dream which told him to go to London where he would meet someone on London Bridge who would bring him his fortune. He did indeed meet a stranger who mocked John on hearing of the dream, saying, 'If I were to believe in dreams, I'd be a fool like you. Recently I dreamt that in Swaffham lived a man called Chapman, and in his garden, buried under a tree lay a treasure.' Undeterred, John rushed home and started digging and, sure enough, found a pot of gold! There is undoubtedly something behind this story because there was a wealthy trader called Chapman in Swaffham who made substantial contributions to the cost of the parish church in the 15th century. This is well worth a visit to admire its harmonious proportions and the outstanding chestnut and oak hammerbeam roof, covered with a squadron of lifesize angels. On one of the pew ends is a model of John Chapman. During the Regency period Swaffham was a fashionable place where the Norfolk gentry used to congregate to attend concerts, balls and soire®es and there are some attractive buildings from this period.

6. Recross the Market Square towards the church and on the far side turn left. At some traffic lights continue ahead along Station Street. Bear right, down Northwell Pool Road. When the road bends right, continue ahead, passing to the left of Northwell Pool.

7. Cross the road at the far end of the pool and turn right for a few yards. Turn left up some steps and follow the path up onto the railway embankment. At the top, turn right along the line of the disused railway taking the left fork. Follow the path to a track and turn right to a road.

This is part of the railway that ran from King's Lynn to Dereham. It was started in 1846 by the Lynn and Dereham Railway which later became part of the Great Eastern Railway. Freight services stopped in 1966 and the passenger trains ceased in 1968.

8. Turn left to the A47 and cross it to Sporle Road, a few yards to the right. Walk along this lane for about ½ mile.

9. Turn right along a tiny track signed 'Grange Farm'. This is the Peddars Way again. Pass the farm and continue across the A47, back to the start.

Walk 2
CASTLE ACRE

*The lovely rolling countryside near Castle Acre is the location of this
superb walk which is highly recommended. It starts near West Acre with a
gentle climb to a level ridge path with extensive views. The route then drops
down through South Acre to the river Nar, crossed at a pretty ford, before
a short climb to Castle Acre with its interesting fortifications and a rose
covered teashop. The return passes the ruins of Castle Acre Priory, well
worth a visit, before wending its way through attractive woodland back to
the start. Although this walk is the longest in this book, the going is easy.
There is much of interest to see and time should be allowed to enjoy the
attractive countryside.*

 The Church Gate Tea Room in Castle Acre, next to the church, is a
charming traditional teashop covered with climbing roses. There are some
tables outside. They serve a variety of delicious cakes together with an

attractive selection for a light lunch, including baguettes, filled jacket potatoes, salads and Welsh rarebit. There is a very tempting choice of desserts. The Church Gate is open every day except Monday between 10.30 am and 5 pm in summer but check when they are open in winter. Telephone: 01760 755551. Website:www.churchgatecastleacre.co.uk

When the teashop is closed there are two pubs in Castle Acre, both serving food, and a restaurant.

DISTANCE: 6½ miles.
MAP: OS Explorer 236 King's Lynn, Downham Market & Swaffham.
STARTING POINT: The large parking area on a minor road near West Acre (GR 788150).
HOW TO GET THERE: From the A47 at Narborough take a minor road signed 'West Acre 2½ Castle Acre 5'. Continue along this road for 2½ miles over two crossroads. As the road bends sharply right there is a large parking area on the left which is the start of the walk.
ALTERNATIVE STARTING POINT: If you want to visit the teashop at the beginning or end of your walk, start in Castle Acre where there are places to park on the main street by the green. You will then begin the walk at point 7.

THE WALK
1. Return to the road and turn right for ¼ mile.

The ruins you can see across the fields to your right are of West Acre Priory, built in 1100 by the Augustinians on a scale to rival that of neighbouring Castle Acre Priory, passed later in the walk. They are mainly on private land.

2. When the hedge on the left ends, turn left on a track along the right-hand side of a field, soon passing under power pylons. Follow the track uphill as it climbs gently with attractive views opening up to a T-junction at the top.

3. Turn left. Follow the track in the same direction for about 1½ miles, crossing two tracks.

A constant feature of this part of the walk, somewhat detracting from the view of this very attractive countryside, are the power lines and their supporting pylons. Power distribution cables can be buried underground, of course, but this is vastly more expensive than lines and pylons and is therefore only done in exceptional areas such as National Parks.

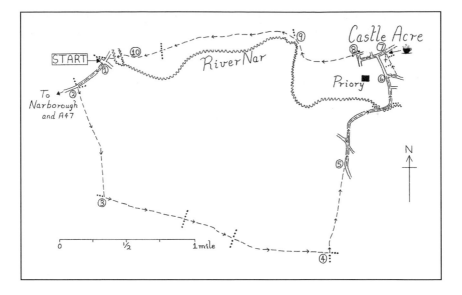

4. At the third crosstrack turn left, climbing slightly with a wood on the right. The track soon starts to go downhill; follow it to a road.

5. Continue in the same direction along the road. After 270 yards, on a left-hand bend, take the second lane on the right, signed 'Ford' and 'Unsuitable for Motors'. Follow this down across the river and up the other side, ignoring the first lane on the right.

6. Turn right along the second lane on the right, Chimney Street. Turn left along a track next to Providence Cottage and continue through the churchyard to the teashop next door.

Castle Acre is an exceptionally attractive village, officially recognised when it was declared the first Conservation Area in Norfolk in 1971. Prehistoric people valued the hilltop position above the water meadows of the Nar valley and the Romans came this way - Peddars Way, a long distance path based on a Roman road, runs through the village (see walk 1). The first castle was built by William de Warenne, an ally of William the Conqueror. Excavations have shown that this was essentially a house surrounded by a ditch and bank and it was not until the 1140s, during the Civil War between King Stephen and Queen Matilda, that it was transformed into a serious defensive structure. The ground floor doors and windows were blocked off and extensive thick curtain walls and earthworks constructed. The castle was never attacked and was virtually abandoned by 1200, providing the local people with an excellent source of building stone. Today only the gateway and earthworks remain but these, together with the fact that much of the present village is built within the bailey of the castle, give some idea of its size.

7. After exploring Castle Acre return along the road past the teashop and church and continue, passing the entrance to Castle Acre Priory on the left.

This extensive priory was founded in 1090 by Warenne's son as a daughter house of the Cluniac Priory of St Pancras at Lewes. The abbey church was built to the same ground plan as the mother church in Burgundy and the west front, surviving almost to its original height, brings home its size. Despite this magnificent scale, there were only 25 or 30 monks living here in the Middle Ages. The prior lived in considerable state, his house having a bath and built in washbasin, so he enjoyed considerably more mod cons than most people at that time. Castle Acre was on the pilgrims' route to Walsingham and as a rival attraction was able to offer them the arm of St Philip. In 1536 this life was swept away with the Dissolution of the monasteries. The prior's house was lived in for a time but most of the priory became another source of building materials. The priory is open every day between 10 am and 5 pm from April to October; in winter it is open at weekends between 10 am and 4 pm. There is an excellent taped tour included in the admission price but you need to allow about an hour for the visit (telephone: 01760 755394).

8. As the road bends right, turn left along a track, signed 'West Acre 1.5 miles' for ½ mile.

9. Just after the track approaches the river Nar, turn left through a kissing gate, on a path way marked 'Nar Valley Way'. This delightful path eventually enters woodland at a small wooden kissing-gate. Continue through the wood, crossing a track, until you leave it again at a metal gate.

Norfolk County Council is to be commended for the care it takes of its footpaths and it is diligent in combining them into various published Ways. This one is 34 miles long and extends from King's Lynn to Gressenhall, being contained almost entirely within the watershed of the river Nar. It is difficult to imagine now but in the past this unspectacular river was navigable from the Wash to Castle Acre, one reason for the importance of the site.

10. Follow the path across a field and two footbridges to a lane. Turn left, back to the start.

Walk 3
SANDRINGHAM

This is a lovely woodland walk exploring part of the Sandringham estate and venturing from there onto Dersingham Common. The whole route is a symphony of beautiful trees, including some magnificent old pines, it is truly a walk for all seasons. In May, the rhododendrons are in bloom, in autumn the fiery colours set the woods alight and in winter hoar frost or snow turn the trees into majestic white giants. Unusually for Norfolk, the walk passes a great viewpoint with a vista across the forest to the sparkling sea beyond. While by no means completely flat, this is not a challenging expedition and can easily be combined with a visit to the house and gardens, when they are open.

The eating facilities at Sandringham Visitor Centre are in two parts. The Terrace Coffee Shop offers sandwiches or hot filled rolls, generous slices of cake, scones or toasted teacakes with cinnamon butter. The main restaurant serves lunch between noon and 3pm and the menu reflects the changing seasons. The management team are very aware of their responsibility to the environment. Everything is sourced as locally as possible and some produce comes from the Sandringham vegetable garden. This is assisted by 'Big Hannah', a machine that turns suitable waste into compost for the garden. They are open throughout the year from 9.30am until 4pm. Telephone: 01485 544548. Website: www.sandringhamestate.co.uk

DISTANCE: 3½ miles
MAP: OS Explorer 250 Norfolk Coast West.
STARTING POINT: Informal parking area near the start of the Scenic Drive. GR 678280
HOW TO GET THERE: From the A149, Kings Lynn Hunstanton road, three miles north of its junction with the A148, take a road east signed 'Sandringham 1¼' to an informal parking area on the right after about 300 yards.
ALTERNATIVE STARTING POINT: If you wish to visit the teashop at the beginning or end of your walk, start at the Visitor Centre for Sandringham Country Park where there is ample parking. The teashop is in the Visitor Centre. You will then start the walk at point 8.

THE WALK
1. Facing the road turn right along the road for about 70 yards then turn left along a surfaced drive, signed 'Country Park Scenic Drive', shortly passing through some metal gates. (For a great view over the forest to the sea beyond take the second track on the left to a viewing platform then return to the drive.) Continue along the drive as far as a wide, grassy ride on the right.

The Sandringham estate is the private property of the Queen. In 1968, she expressed the wish that everybody should be able to enjoy the beautiful woods and heaths so some 600 acres were designated as a country park, freely open to all.

2. At the end of the ride turn sharp left, ignoring a path leading half left and follow the path downhill, helped by steps at the steepest point. Follow the main path round to the right and continue for ½ mile to something of a clearing with several paths leading from it and, at the time of writing, a post with number 15 on it.

3. Cross a plank bridge across a ditch on the left then follow the main path ahead eventually to climb and cross another plank bridge.

17

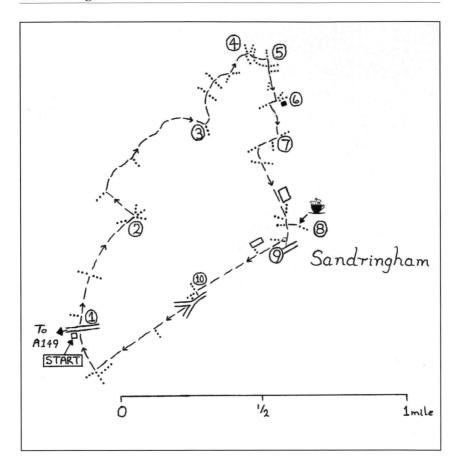

4. Some 20 yards after crossing this second bridge turn right. Almost immediately keep ahead over a cross path to arrive at a T-junction.

5. Turn right and follow the path to an open area in front of a fence and buildings.

6. Turn right for 50 yards to a plank bridge then continue for 10 yards. Turn left over yet another plank bridge (not ahead, also over a plank bridge). Follow the narrow but clear path as it wends through woods to a T-junction with a broad path.

☕ **7.** Turn right for 150 yards, ignoring an obvious path on the left after 40 yards. Turn left and continue across a drive to the visitor

18

An alternative way to explore the estate

centre and teashop on the left. The house and gardens are a short distance away: follow the signs (and crowds).

Albert Edward, Prince of Wales, the future King Edward VII, bought Sandringham House with its estate at the time of some 7,000 acres as a country home in the spring of 1862. He had just turned 21 and moved in with his new wife, Princess Alexandra of Denmark, three weeks after their marriage in 1863. It soon became clear that the old house was too cramped for the couple's growing family and so was demolished to make way for a new house, completed in 1870 and very up-to-date with gas lighting, flushing water closets and showers. It has remained the much-loved country home of the royal family ever since. For example, King George V wrote, "Dear old Sandringham, the place I love better than anywhere else in the world." This affection continues to the present day, as is evident from the amount of time that the Queen and her family spend here. It is owned by them privately and is not part of the Crown Estate. Edward VIII had inherited it from his father and when he abdicated, George VI had to buy it from him. King Edward VII first opened the superb gardens at Sandringham to the public in 1908, and in 1930 the Museum was opened with an admission charge of 3d. The Queen opened the House to the public in 1977, Silver Jubilee year. The house, gardens and museum are open from March to November. See www.sandringhamestate.co.uk for more information. Telephone 01485 545408.

8. Turn right out of the teashop then turn left at a cross track, crossing the end of a wide, grassy drive. Take the third surfaced track on the right, just before a road, for 30 yards.

9. Bear left on a wide path parallel with the road some 50 yards to the left. Follow this for ½ mile to a major track on the right.

10. Turn left at this point to the road. Turn right to almost immediately reach a road junction then continue ahead on a wide, grassy drive between the two roads. Walk to the end of the ride.

11. At the end of the grassy area two paths lead ahead: take the one on the right that soon leads through trees to a broad cross path. Turn right and follow the path to a road. Turn left back to the start. (Keep more or less ahead if you started at the Visitor Centre.)

Walk 4
CLEY MARSH and CLEY-NEXT-THE-SEA

*E*ast Anglia *is famous for the richness of its bird life and along the North Norfolk coast is a chain of nature reserves protecting feeding and breeding grounds. Cley Marsh is one of these and has the distinction of being the oldest in the country. This short and straightforward walk visits this mecca for bird watchers and the charming old port of Cley-next-the-Sea. The path around the reserve is either a recognised public footpath or a permitted path which you can use freely. If you wish to penetrate into the marsh and visit the hides you must buy a permit. These are available at the Visitor Centre – see below.*

 Cookes of Cley is a traditional establishment based in a pebble-faced house at the east end of the village. There are tables in the pretty, sheltered garden as well as inside. For tea there is an ever-changing selection of cakes served in generous slices as well as cream teas. Possibilities for lunch include fresh local crab and mussels, when available, as well as excellent filled rolls or delicious homemade soup and bread. Lunch is served between noon and 3.00pm and they are open from 10.00am until 5.30pm during the holiday season. In the winter Cookes is just open at the weekend. Telephone 01263 740776. Website: www.cookes-of-cley.co.uk

The Visitor Centre at Cley Marshes where this walk starts is a stunning modern building with a turf roof that has a cafe serving snacks and cakes. It has many features designed to reduce its impact on the environment such as a wind turbine, solar panels and ground source heat pump and rainwater is collected and recycled for use in flushing the loos. Another notable feature is the enormous window overlooking the reserve. The cafe is open every day from the beginning of March until the end of October between 10am and 4pm. Telephone: 01263 740008. Website: www.norfolkwildlifetrust.org.uk/cley

DISTANCE: 3 miles
MAP: OS Explorer 251 Norfolk Coast Central
STARTING POINT: Cley Marsh Visitor Centre car park (GR 053441)
HOW TO GET THERE: The Visitor Centre is on the south side of the A149, North Norfolk coast road, a couple of hundred yards to the east of a minor road to Newton, just outside Cley-next-the-Sea.
ALTERNATIVE STARTING POINT: Parking in Cley is very limited and the village car park is at the other end of the village from Cookes.

THE WALK
Facing onto the North Sea, the North Norfolk coast is an evolving landscape of dunes, marshes and intertidal flats which is internationally recognised for its wildlife, especially birds. Cley (pronounced Cly) Marshes was the first nature reserve to be acquired by the oldest county Naturalists Trust. It was bought by a syndicate of ornithologists led by the founder of Norfolk Wildlife Trust, Dr. Sydney Long, in 1926 and is one of the foremost sites for bird watching in the UK. At the time of writing there is an appeal to raise £1million to complete the purchase of a further 143 acres. The information centre at the rear of the car park is worth a visit before starting this walk to learn something of the history and management of this important Nature Reserve as well as enjoying a cup of tea.

1. Take the path from the car park to the road. Cross the road and go ahead to a T junction. Turn right and continue parallel with the road as far as a second, smaller car park.

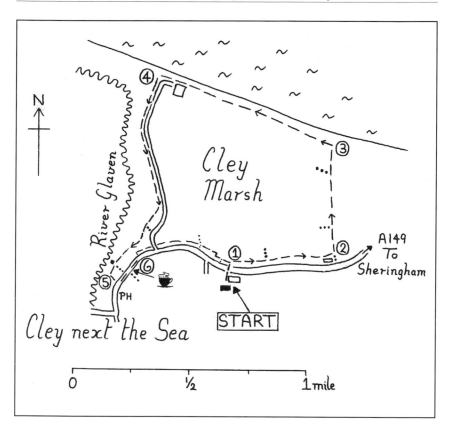

2. Turn left on a path along the top of a bank and follow it as far as a high shingle bank.

Over the past 150 years over 300 species of birds have been recorded here. This diversity is partly explained by the range of habitats found. There are both saltwater and freshwater marshes as well as grazing marsh and reedbeds. Water levels are carefully managed to maintain this variety. The reeds are cut in rotation and sold for thatch. This encourages new growth and the development of areas of reedbed of different ages attractive to a multiplicity of species. Bittern shelter in the reeds and the males boom can often be heard, particularly in the early morning or evening. The variety of waders is astonishing including rarities like Kentish plovers and Temminck's stint as well as sandpipers and redshank. Wintering species are equally varied and include teal, wigeon, shovelor and snow buntings. Another reason for the wide range of species recorded is Cley Marshes' position, jutting out into the North Sea. This means that migrating birds blown off course find landfall here and

23

all sorts of rarities turn up. When this happens the great army of "twitchers" or obsessive bird watchers are alerted by their phone hot line and flock to see the bird so they can cross it off their list

3. Turn left along the shingle bank as far as the beach car park.

The shingle bank provides some protection from the sea but it can be breached by tidal surges as occurred in 1953, 1978, 1992 and 1996. After the latest of these in March 1996 the reserve was under several feet of water for some days. Some of the old hides were swept away as were some stretches of newly laid boardwalk.

4. Turn left on a path signed 'Cley-next-the-sea 1m' to walk parallel with the road leading to the beach car park. Continue along it as it starts to veer away from the road towards a windmill. Follow the path, passing the mill on your right and continue along the track round to the left to the road in Cley.

5. To explore Cley, turn right. To continue with the route, turn left to the teashop on the right.

Cley was a busy port in the Middle Ages exporting wool to the Low Countries and its prosperity is shown by the grandiose parish church of St, Margaret's with its high nave and richly carved pew ends. Natural silting and deliberate land reclamation have left the village half a mile from the sea and accessible only to small craft: the windmill now looks out over marsh where once it stood on the quay side.

6. Turn right out of the teashop. At the 30mph sign take a permitted path on the left parallel with the road back to the start.

Walk 5
BEESTON REGIS and
PRETTY CORNER

The area between Cromer and Sheringham is relatively hilly for Norfolk – a wooded ridge runs parallel to the sea and rises to over 300 feet above sea level. This walk starts near the sea at Beeston Regis and visits its ancient priory before climbing through the woods to the aptly named Pretty Corner for tea. More energetic than many of the walks in this book, the route is highly recommended for its fine views and attractive woodland paths. You can be sure your efforts will be rewarded with a sustaining tea.

Pretty Corner Tea Gardens certainly lives up to its name with tables scattered round the attractive garden and on a terrace overlooking a sunken area with a pond and small fountain. There are some tables inside for less clement weather. Delicious cakes and other teatime goodies are served and salads, sandwiches or baguettes together with soup are available for a light lunch. If you are hungry there is a choice of full meals including pasta dishes or Cajun chicken complemented by traditional puddings. They open from April to October between 10.30 am and 5 pm, every day except Tuesday. There has been a tea garden here since 1926 when it consisted of a wooden pavilion. There was no water supply on the site at that time and each day water had to be collected from a spring-fed well in Upper Sheringham. There was also no electricity supply so cooking was done with a wood-burning stove and lighting was provided by paraffin lamps. The owners at that time became widely renowned for their home-made chocolates and sweets, which won a number of awards and were even exported to France. Telephone: 01263 822766 Website: www.prettycornerteagardens.com

There is no alternative source of refreshment on this route.

DISTANCE: 4 miles.

MAP: OS Explorer 252 Norfolk Coast East.

STARTING POINT: The walk starts at Beeston Regis where there is a large parking area made from a bend in the A149 that has been straightened out (GR 166426).

HOW TO GET THERE: The A149 is the North Norfolk coast road. The parking area is on the south side of the road just after the Beeston Regis sign when approaching from Sheringham and just before the Sheringham sign when coming from the east.

ALTERNATIVE STARTING POINT: If you want to visit the teashop at the beginning or end of your walk, start at the public car park at Pretty Corner (GR 153412) signed from the A1082 just outside Sheringham. The teashop is about ¼ mile from the car park. From the car park, take a path on the right. Bear right after 20 yards and follow a path roughly parallel with the lane to the tea garden. You will then start the walk at point 9.

THE WALK

Note: There are many formal and informal paths in Pretty Corner Woods. Please be sure to follow the route directions carefully.

1. Leave the parking area at the eastern (Beeston) end and turn right along the road for 75 yards. Turn left along a track, branching left after 20 yards along a hedged path. Continue past the ruins of Beeston Regis Priory on the right then turn left along a track. At the end of the track turn right down Church Lane. At the end of the road, in front of the railway, bear right on a waymarked path, to walk by the line. Follow the track as it bends right, away from the railway, at a crossing and continue along it to a road.

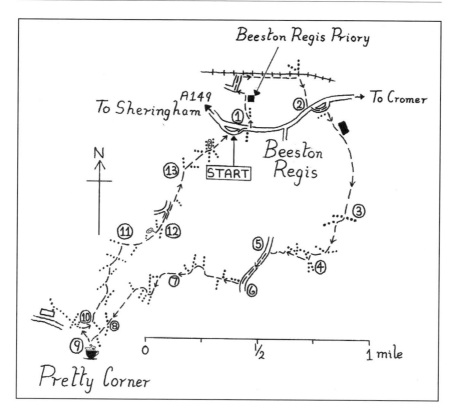

Beeston Regis Priory was founded at the end of the 12th century by Augustinian canons who served as priests for neighbouring parishes. It was on the pilgrimage route to Walsingham and provided accommodation for travellers. Before being suppressed in 1539 during the Dissolution it was said that the canons indulged in 'vicious, carnal and abominable living' but to what extent that was true and how much was propaganda we cannot now say. The priory is in the care of Norfolk County Council and open all the time. Information boards explain what can be seen.

2. Cross the road and turn left for 25 yards then bear right along another straightened bend in the road, signed as the coastal path and 'Roman Camp 1¼m'. After about 150 yards turn right along a gravelled drive to Hall Farm. Continue past some buildings and a small caravan site.

3. When the track forks at a wood, do not take either branch but continue ahead on a path into the wood. Follow the path up through the wood. As it bends right, ignore paths on the left and right to continue on the now level path. After 50 yards, similarly ignore a further path on the right at a left-hand bend.

The Cromer Ridge runs parallel with the coast from Sidestrand westwards to Bodham where it turns south-west towards Holt and becomes less distinct. Along its length is the highest point in Norfolk, 328 feet above sea level, at Roman Camp close to the highest part of this walk. The ridge is a recent phenomenon, geologically speaking. It was formed in the last Ice Age as a push moraine. Ice moving from the north forced up the layers of rock in front of it and covered the fold with a thick layer of sand and gravel. The north slope, the direction from which the push came, is a steep scarp slope giving wonderful views from the summit.

4. After a further 30 yards the path comes to a complex junction at a fence corner. Turn right here to walk with the fence on your left. Follow the path by the fence which eventually drops steeply down to a lane. There are several branches on the right before it starts to descend. Many lead to lovely spots to rest and admire the great views over to the sea but if you are tempted away, do be sure to return to the path by the fence.

5. Turn left along the lane for 350 yards.

6. Turn right along a track signed 'Sheringwood'. Follow the main track as it eventually bends right and forks left. Ignore all the side tracks which lead to houses hidden in the woods. At the entrance to Bracken Hill, fork left then left again to pass the entrance to Robin Hill. Continue ahead, soon leaving the last of the houses, Beechwood, behind.

7. The track is now more of a path with a boundary fence on the left. Follow the path along the valley side for about 150 yards until it descends a little to a crosspath then continue uphill on the opposite side of the little valley to a broad crosspath after 20 yards. Turn right. Take the right option at the first junction and the left one at a second junction. Follow the path as it climbs gently through the woods.

8. At a crosspath by a carving of a teapot and cup continue in the same direction on a smaller path. Follow this to the gate into the tea garden grounds and follow the signs bearing right to the tea garden itself.

28

(Note: the route described goes through the grounds of the tea garden. If you don't want to visit the tea garden or if you do this walk when the tea garden is closed and the gate into the grounds is locked, turn right in front of the gates to follow a path up by the fence to rejoin the route.)

9. From the terrace go down into the sunken garden and take a path up a ramp to the right of the building to leave by a different gate. Follow the path ahead through the woods to a T-junction with a crosspath.

10. Turn right. Ignore all side paths and continue ahead through the woods, gently downhill. Eventually the path comes close to, but does not touch, a track on the right and then veers away left uphill. Soon after this the path comes to a T-junction with a crosspath. Turn right and carry on down through the woods, ignoring a path on the right then up a small rise. At the top turn right, downhill once more, to a T-junction with a crosspath.

11. Turn right. Ignore all paths to left and right and pass a pond on the left to arrive at another T-junction.

12. Turn left and follow the main track down past some waterworks to a short stretch of road. When this joins a residential street continue ahead in the same direction on an occasionally surfaced path parallel with the street.

13. Watch for a gap in the hedge on the left opposite house number 2 then bear right on a waymarked path. Follow this path across the common, turning right at a T-junction then crossing a small bridge. Continue ahead at a crosspaths by a small and very attractive pond, back to the start.

This is Sheringham Common. Contrary to what many people believe, commons are not owned by the public. Common land is owned by someone but differs from ordinary land because some people other than the owner have rights over it. These are of various kinds; estovers is the right to pick up fallen timber for fuel and pannage is the right to graze pigs, for example. Commoners may have rights to graze animals but these are often not exercised because changes in farming practice make them uneconomic. In that case commons which were open land can quickly become invaded by scrub and eventually trees unless management is undertaken to prevent this.

Walk 6
BLICKLING

Blickling Park, owned by the National Trust, is freely open to the public every day from dawn to dusk. This walk is a pleasant blend of woods, fields and attractive parkland and passes all the main features, including the outstanding Jacobean hall where the usual excellent National Trust tea room is to be found. The return is along the side of a lake.

 The National Trust can be relied on for a good tea and this is no exception. The restaurant at Blickling Hall serves the usual splendid selection of cakes, scones and other teatime goodies. Lunches are available between 12 noon and 2 pm and feature delicious soup, ploughman's with two cheeses, ham or pâté, salads and a daily selection of hot meals. There are some tables outside in the courtyard, through the restaurant. The restaurant is open every day from mid February to early November and closes Monday to Wednesday in the winter. Telephone: 01263 733084 Website: www.nationaltrust.org.uk/blickling-estate

When the teashop is closed the Bucks Arms, also owned by the National Trust, serves bar lunches.

DISTANCE: 4 miles.

MAP: OS Explorer 252 Norfolk Coast East.

STARTING POINT: Park Farm car park, Blickling Estate (GR 179296).

HOW TO GET THERE: From the centre of Aylsham just off the A140 between Norwich and Cromer, follow the signs to Blickling Hall. Take the second road signed 'Ingworth 1' on the right (not the first, Petersons Lane) for about ¾ mile. Turn left signed 'Itteringham' and continue for ¾ mile to a farm on the left and turn left on a track to a car park, which is not signed at the time of writing.

ALTERNATIVE STARTING POINT: If you want to visit the teashop at the beginning or end of your walk, start in the main car park for Blickling Hall on the B1354. The restaurant is signed from the car park. You will then start the walk at point 7.

THE WALK

1. Leave the car park by a path at the far end and walk to a lake.

In 1616 Sir Henry Hobart, Chief Justice of the Common Pleas to James I, bought the Blickling estate and built the outstanding house, one of the last great Jacobean mansions to be constructed in England. Detailed accounts of the building of the house exist but there is much less information about the park at that time. There were originally two deer parks, one belonging to the Bishops of Norwich and the other to the owners of the manor, but they had been united into one by the time Hobart acquired the estate. In the 17th century there may have been a series of fishponds on the site of the lake but it had been excavated by the time a detailed map was drawn in 1729 when Sir John Hobart was undertaking major changes in the park. The lake was increased in 1762 then shortened again 100 years later in 1863. It is now about ½ mile long and curved to create the illusion of a broad river from the house. Well stocked with coarse fish, it is popular with anglers.

The estate stayed in the Hobart family and their descendants for 300 years but they were somewhat impoverished in the late 16th century and this ensured the Jacobean mansion survived. By the time the family became prosperous again in the mid 18th century, the Jacobean style was seen as romantic, so many parts of the original building were retained rather than swept aside as old fashioned. Sir James Hobart was created Earl of Buckingham in 1745 and the 2nd Earl was responsible for many features of the hall today.

31

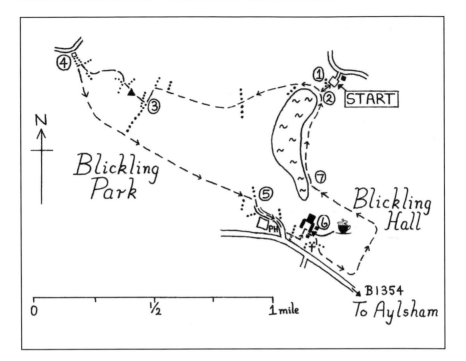

2. Turn right to walk round the end and then leave the lake to go ahead on a path marked by a blue arrow. There is soon an excellent view of the hall down the lake. Continue ahead at a crosstrack and follow the path round a field and into a wood, the route marked by red and blue arrows. Continue as far as the Mausoleum, a triangular structure, on the right.

The pyramid is 45 feet square at the base and built of Portland stone. Inspired by the tomb of Gaius Cestius in Rome, it was built to house the tombs of the 2nd Earl of Buckingham and his two Countesses.

3. Turn right to pass the Mausoleum. Take the path leading from the rear. Stay on the wider, main path as it meanders through the woods, eventually going downhill.

4. At the bottom of the hill, within sight of a gate, car park and house, turn left on a cut-through for 25 yards to a broad cross track. Turn left and follow the track through a wooden field gate. Stay on this track through the park.

As you walk along the track, look across the park to the right for a castellated building. This is the Tower, built in 1773 as a kind of grandstand overlooking the 'Raceground'. It was originally whitewashed and is now a private house.

☕ **5.** At a T-junction with a crosstrack turn right out of the park then bear left to pass the Bucks Arms. Turn left down the main drive to the hall to reach the restaurant in the buildings on the right.

During its long history Blickling has changed hands many times and soldiers, diplomats and judges have all left their mark. In the 14th century a moated manor house was built by Sir Nicholas Dagworth, Captain of Aquitaine under Richard II. In 1431 it was bought by Sir John Fastolfe, one of the models for Shakespeare's Falstaff. He sold it to a prote®ge® called Geoffrey Boleyn whose family owned it up to the time of the execution of his great-granddaughter, Anne, second wife of King Henry VIII and mother of Elizabeth I. Local tradition holds that Anne was born at Blickling and spent part of her childhood here. It is said that she returns in a ghostly coach, holding her head on her lap, on the anniversary of her execution on 19 May 1536.

After the estate was bought by the Hobarts, who became the Earls of Buckingham, it descended through the female line to the Marquess of Lothian. The 11th Marquess left it to the National Trust when he died in 1940. During the Second World War it was used as the officers' mess for RAF Oulton Street and one officer recalls the North Sea was warm in comparison with the bath water.

The partly 13th-century church by the entrance contains some notable monuments to this succession of colourful characters. Sir Nicholas Dagworth is commemorated in an outstanding military brass and there are several Boleyns and a brass to a poor unfortunate Ann Wood, who died giving birth to the twins she holds.

Do visit the hall and garden if you have time (telephone: 01263 733084). The hall's most outstanding feature is the Long Gallery, originally built for indoor exercise in bad weather and hung with pictures. The plasterwork ceiling is its greatest glory with 31 panels of heraldic motifs and symbolic figures interspersed between a dense network of decorative moulding. All this for just over ªfifty originally! In the mid 18th century it became the library and now has over 12,000 books, some of them very old, rare and valuable. The Long Gallery leads into the scarcely less impressive Peter the Great Room. The 2nd Earl of Buckingham served as ambassador to Catherine the Great and she gave him a tapestry showing the Tsar riding into battle against the Swedes. On his return, he had this room redesigned to take his precious souvenir and later added the portraits by Gainsborough of himself, draped in ermine, and his second wife. There is also a picture of his sister, Countess of Suffolk, one of the most dazzling society ladies of her time – friend of the intelligentsia and mistress of George II.

6. After tea go through an arch in a yew hedge on the tea room side and through a courtyard. Leave the courtyard to the right, cross a drive and take a path leading left, signed 'Start of waymarked walks'. Follow the path ahead then left and left again round the garden to the lake.

This path gives many glimpses into the garden which has been here since the Jacobean house was built but has changed and evolved with the passing centuries up to modern times. For example, the colourful herbaceous borders were planted in the 1930s by Norah Lindsay and reflect the ideas of the great Gertrude Jekyll. The woodland garden was badly damaged in the 1987 storm and has seen substantial replanting. The orangery, close to the path, was built in 1782 when imported oranges were fabulously expensive and so the rich grew their own under glass, heated by braziers.

7. Turn right along the lake. As you approach the end, turn right to retrace your steps back to the start.

Walk 7
BRANCASTER and
BURNHAM DEEPDALE

*T*he North Norfolk coast is an Area of Outstanding Natural Beauty, much
loved for the wild remoteness of the salt marshes that fringe the coast and
the abundant bird life they support as well as the many attractive and
historic villages. This interesting walk explores all these elements. It starts
in Brancaster, where a Roman fort once protected the coast. The route
climbs gently to one of the highest spots around for a wonderful view across
the marshes to the sea beyond. The hill is crowned with a gorse-covered
common, a lovely spot to linger on a sunny day when the gorse is in bloom
and the birds in song. The route then drops down to Burnham Deepdale
where an excellent teashop offers refreshment before a two-mile walk
beside the marsh gives a close-up view of this special landscape and leads
back to Brancaster.

Deepdale Café says its philosophy is to serve good food in comfortable, clean surroundings and they fully succeed in that aim. The extensive menu is enticing and ranges from sandwiches, including fresh crab in season, through salads and omelettes to a daily selection of full meals such as, on my visit, grilled sardines in a tasty tomato sauce. There is also an excellent selection of tempting cakes and desserts. Open every day from 8 am, when breakfast is served to campers from the adjacent campsite and backpackers' hostel, until 4 pm. As well as the lively modern interior, there are some tables outside. Telephone: 01485 211055. Website: www.deepdalecafe.co.uk

DISTANCE: 5 miles.

MAP: OS Explorer 250 Norfolk Coast West.

STARTING POINT: London Street, Brancaster, where there are several places to leave a car without causing obstruction (GR 774439).

HOW TO GET THERE: Brancaster is on the A149, North Norfolk coast road. London Street is a few yards to the east of The Ship pub.

ALTERNATIVE STARTING POINT: If you wish to visit the teashop at the beginning or end of your walk, start in Burnham Deepdale where there is some parking, including a lay-by across the road from the teashop. The teashop is on the A149. You will then start the walk at point 4.

THE WALK

1. Return to the main road and turn left to walk out of Brancaster. Just before the speed limit deregulation sign, at Stockings Lane on the left, cross the road to a footway on the right and continue ahead for 300 yards.

The field on the left of the road was the site of a Roman fort called Branodunum. Towards the end of the second century AD this coast came under attack from Angles, Saxons and Frisians from northern Germany and Holland. The Roman response was to build a series of forts along the coast and this was one. It was surrounded by a 10-ft-wide wall backed by an earthen rampart enclosing an area of about six acres and fronted by a single ditch. In those days it faced the open sea rather than being about a mile inland, illustrating how this coast has changed. As usual, it attracted a civilian settlement so there has been a community here since those days. The stone-built Saxon shore fort was probably the third on the site, replacing earlier wooden structures. The first is thought to date from the time of Boudicca, when the local Iceni people rebelled against the occupation and almost defeated them. There is little to see today since the stone was reused and some of the material can be seen in Brancaster church.

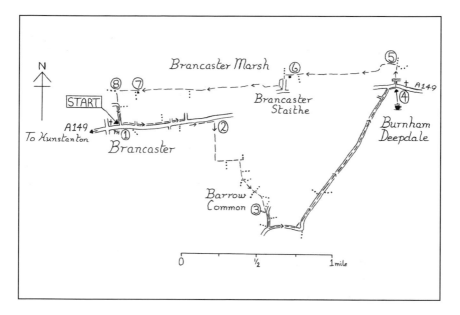

2. Turn right on a wide hedged track. Follow the track round a left hand bend, ignore a track on the right. Just before the track enters a field turn right on a hedged, grassy path. Go through a gate across the path and press on across Barrow Common, ignoring all paths to left and right, to arrive at a fork where the branch to the left is shortly barred by a wooden barrier. Bear right, downhill, to a lane.

3. Turn right to a junction. Turn left and walk along the lane to Burnham Deepdale. Turn right at the main road to find the teashop almost immediately on the right.

There are seven Burnhams in total, taking their name from the little river Burn. The church across the road is worth a visit for its three outstanding features - its Saxon round tower, which is about 950 years old, the Norman font, and its collection of medieval glass. The square font depicts a figure for each month of the year from a farming man's point of view. For example February shows a person with his feet up before the fire. The collection of medieval glass is rich and varied: the windows in the porch contain delightful medieval faces of the sun and moon.

4. Cross the main road and walk along The Drove opposite. At the end continue ahead along a track, signed 'To Norfolk Coast path', to a National Trust sign.

Boats at Brancaster Staithe.

5. Turn left on the coast path, signed 'Brancaster Staithe 1m'.

This coastline, one of the most unspoilt in England, is in a state of constant evolution under the influences of tide and weather so what you see today is not what was here a century ago nor what will be here in another hundred years. Wind and waves have forged a series of shingle ridges, sandflats, dunes and marshes that are of global importance for wildlife, especially birds (see Walk 4, page 21). It is protected both as an Area of Outstanding Natural Beauty and by an unbroken series of nature reserves stretching from Holme to Weybourne. A special landscape with such enormous wildlife interest is in danger of being loved to death and the management strategy has to try to balance the demands of recreation and development with the needs of conservation.

6. At Brancaster Staithe, carry on past the working boats and sailing club then turn left along a track towards a red and white buoy for 50 yards. Now turn right to carry on along the coast path, waymarked with white acorns.

In the 18th century, Brancaster Staithe was an important port trading in coal and grain. Changes in the size of boats, the coming of the railway and silting of the harbour have meant this commercial traffic has died and now it is mostly pleasure craft, though whelks are dredged from the seabed offshore.

7. As the buildings of Brancaster start on the left, go over a stile by a house with a round tower topped by a ship weathervane. Ignore the first track on the left and press on along the coast path for 200 yards to a second track.

8. Turn left through a gate and walk along the track, which becomes London Street where this walk started.

Walk 8
HOW HILL and LUDHAM

Tbis exceptionally varied walk captures all the characteristics of this part of East Anglia. Starting at How Hill Nature Reserve, the route begins along the bank of the River Ant, busy with river traffic in the summer season, and then makes its way to the ancient community of Ludham and an outstanding teashop. The return uses exceptionally well maintained field paths and finally climbs How Hill back to the start. How Hill may be noteworthy in this flat landscape but since it is only about 40 feet high, its ascent does not require much effort!

Alfresco is the end property of a row of charming thatched cottages in Ludham, opposite the church. It has a small but delightful flower-filled garden at the back and serves an outstanding selection of delicious and sometimes unusual cakes, all made on the premises. For lunch there is a range of sandwiches, filled jackets and daily specials. It is open every day from Mothering Sunday weekend to the end of October half term between 10 am and 5pm. Telephone: 01692 678384

An alternative for tea is The Wayfarers at Ludham Bridge (point 3), a friendly and cheerful establishment that has won awards as the best Broads café and is geared to the needs of the many boat people on the river. It serves good cakes and a most satisfying all day breakfast. It also has a garden. Open 9am to 4pm every day between April and November. Telephone: 01692 630322.

DISTANCE: 5½ miles
MAP: OS Outdoor Leisure 40 The Broads
STARTING POINT: How Hill car park (GR 372189)
HOW TO GET THERE: From the A1062 Potter Heigham-Horning road ¾ mile east of Ludham Bridge over the River Ant, take a minor road north signed 'How Hill'. After ½ mile take the second lane left. The car park is on the left and signed. Use the one for Toad Hole Cottage and Wildlife Walks.
ALTERNATIVE STARTING POINT: If you want to visit the teashop at the beginning or end of your walk, start in Ludham where there is some parking by the church. You will then start the walk at point 7.

THE WALK

How Hill Nature Reserve is owned by the Broads Authority and managed to maintain a diversity of habitats including open water, fen, reed beds, grazing marshes and carr woodland. The How Hill House was built by the Norwich architect Edward Boardman early in the 20th century and remained the family home until the 1960s. It is now an Environmental Study Centre with courses for both adults and children. The lovely gardens are occasionally open to the public and there is a tearoom open on summer weekends.

1. From the car park head half right across the picnic area to a track. Turn left to the river bank then turn left again beside the river, passing Toad Hall Cottage.

It is worth visiting Toad Hall Cottage, a tiny eel catcher's cottage, furnished in period that also serves as an information centre. It is free and open between April and October.

2. Continue on the path as it deviates away from the river bank. Bear right at a fork then ignore paths to right and left to return to the river bank and follow the clear and easy path for about 1½ miles to a bridge.

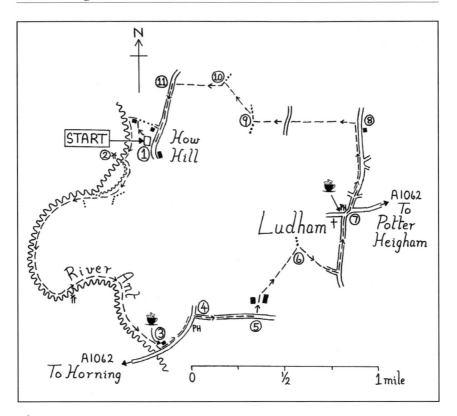

N
↑

START

How
Hill

River Ant

Ludham †

A1062
To
Potter
Heigham

A1062
To Horning

PH

0   ½   1 mile

☕ **3.** Turn left along the footpath beside the road.

4. Just past The Dog Inn turn right along a lane signed 'Hall Common'.

5. After about ¼ mile turn left on a track and follow it between barns and the house of Ludham Hall Farm, then on along the left hand side of a field.

Ludham Hall Farm was one of the three manors in Ludham, once known as Ludham Grange. It was given to nearby St Benet's Abbey by King Canute in AD1019 and was partly destroyed by fire in AD1611. Adjoining it is a chapel, now disused, which was once the chapel of the Bishop of Norwich.

☕ **6.** As the track bends left, turn right on an unsigned path which eventually becomes a surfaced lane. Follow this to a T-junction on the outskirts of Ludham. Turn left and walk through the village to the church. The teashop is opposite.

St. Catherine's is a large and magnificent church for the present size of the community and has some interesting features. Perhaps the most extraordinary is the 15th-century font. On the bowl are carvings of Matthew, Mark, Luke and John while on the base are depictions of the Greenman or Woodwose on one side and the Green Woman on the other side showing how pagan beliefs persisted alongside Christianity. On the right buttress of the south door into the chancel is a mass dial and a hand sticks out of the wall of the south aisle. This once used to hold a bell rope. There is more information available in the church.

7. From the teashop turn left then left again along High Street. Continue out of the village, fortunately there is a good path on the left hand side of the road.

Ludham is an attractive village of thatched cottages built in rows. The name comes from Luda's manor or town and it is thought to be of Saxon origin. The settlement was much influenced by its proximity to St Benet's Abbey, now a desolate ruin in the marshes only accessible on foot. The abbey was first founded in AD800 but then destroyed by marauding Vikings. It was refounded by King Canute, who gave the manor of Ludham to the Abbey in 1019. The Abbey became one of the richest in East Anglia with property in over 70 parishes, as well as substantial interests in the peat industry. Despite its wealth, this monastery had the distinction of being the only one in England to escape the Dissolution. Henry VIII did a deal. He made the last Abbot Bishop of Norwich in 1536 and he handed over the estates of the cathedral and in return was allowed to keep those of the abbey. Even today, the Bishop of Norwich is Abbot of St Benet's, though he has no monks.

8. About 50 yards after an isolated bungalow on the right, turn left on an initially hedged path. When this reaches a lane, continue in the same direction on the opposite side along the right hand side of a field.

9. At the end of the field turn right on a cross path for 60 yards. Turn left through a gap in the hedge and head slightly right across two fields to a grassy path.

10. Turn left.

11. At a lane turn left back to the start.

Walk 9
WINSTON and DEBENHAM

This easy walk explores the charming countryside of one of the prettiest corners of Suffolk. The route includes a couple of gentle climbs and such height as is attained gives lovely views over the rolling landscape with its patchwork of fields and woods. Nestling in this attractive corner is the ancient community of Debenham. It is well worth ensuring you allow time to explore the village as it has a wealth of attractive old buildings testifying to its long history.

 The teashop visited on this walk is particularly appropriate as it is located at a pottery that specialises in making unusual and amusing teapots. Tony and Anita Carter set up their pottery in 1978 and today they design and make collectable teapots, with over 70% of them exported throughout the world. During the week you can watch the teapots being made and painted by hand from the viewing area. The teashop is in an airy, modern conservatory and there are some tables outside in summer. They serve a small selection of delicious cakes and scones, including tasty cheese scones and cream teas. The tea is served in one of the many unusual teapots manufactured on the premises, proving they are practical as well as entertaining. The teashop is open from 9 am until 5.30 pm Monday to Friday, 10.30 am until 4.30 pm on Saturday and bank holidays, but closed on Sundays. When Carter's is closed there are several pubs in Debenham that serve food. Telephone: 01728 861110. Website:www.cartersteapots.com

DISTANCE: 3 miles.

MAP: OS Explorer 211 Bury St Edmunds & Stowmarket.

STARTING POINT: St. Andrew's church, Winston (GR 180616).

HOW TO GET THERE: From the A1120, Stowmarket to Yoxford road, about 10 miles east of Stowmarket, take the B1077 towards Debenham. When the road bends sharp right after about half a mile, continue in the same direction on a minor road, signed 'Winston Hall and church', to a parking area by the church.

ALTERNATIVE STARTING POINT: If you wish to visit the tea shop at the beginning or end of your walk, start in Debenham where there is a small car park on the High Street. You will then start the walk part way through point 7.

THE WALK

If the railway had come to Debenham in the 19th century it would have grown and become more industrial, as did nearby Stowmarket. The village would have reached out and engulfed this little church, and we would now be standing among modern semis or beside a distribution warehouse. But the railway did not reach Debenham, and Debenham did not reach Winston so it remains a pretty little hamlet. The church is a Victorian rebuild, although the tower is still in its original 14th-century slenderness and charm. It is usually locked, though the key-holder lives in one of the cottages nearby.

1. Take a signed path into the churchyard. Walk with the church on the left to find a path at the far side. The start is not obvious but is in line with the end of the church. It soon becomes clear and leads through a strip of woodland to a wooden barrier into a field. Bear half right across the field to a gap in a hedge and continue in the same direction across a second field to a stile onto a road.

2. Turn left along the road.

3. When the road bends sharp left, turn right along a track for 80 yards then turn left along another track. Continue ahead as a track joins on the right to a lane.

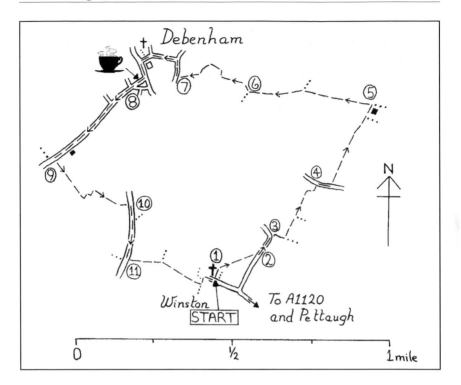

If you had done this walk 200 years ago the landscape would have been quite different. In those days Debenham was known as a centre for dairying. James Cornish, son of a 19th-century vicar of Debenham, wrote of trees being felled and hedges removed until 'our district was entirely grubbed up and transformed into corn land'. Nowadays the views are of a predominantly arable landscape but nonetheless still most attractive.

4. Turn right for 120 yards then left on a signed bridleway along a track, going gently uphill. Continue past farm buildings to a T-junction with a surfaced drive.

5. Turn left along the drive for about ½ mile, passing Crows Hall Cottages then gently downhill to a sharp left hand bend.

This drive leads to Crows Hall, a moated 16th-century brick built hall not generally open to the public. The drive is lined with old oak trees, some showings signs of their age while others are still magnificent. Fortunately, young trees have been planted to replace those about to be overtaken by the ravages of time.

6. Turn right on a signed path along the right hand side of a field. The church at Debenham soon comes into view. Press on along the path round the edge of the field to a way-marked gap in the hedge on the right. Go through the gap and continue towards the village to a lane.

7. Turn right, then take the first lane on the left. Follow this lane into the village. Turn left along the High Street then right along Low Road to the teashop on the right.

The lovely old village of Debenham takes its name from the River Deben, which trickles through the centre of the settlement. There has been a community in this favoured spot since time immemorial. The Saxon kings of East Anglia regularly held court here and an important battle against the Danes was fought nearby in AD 870. Debenham was mentioned in the Domesday Book and some of the oldest buildings are not much younger! Number 56 High Street is said to date from about 1190 and parts of the church are of a similar date, just over a hundred years after Domesday was compiled. The former Ancient Order of the Foresters Chapel, also on the High Street featured as an antiques shop in the TV series Lovejoy. At the junction of Gracechurch Street and the High Street stands the quaint market cross, reputedly built in the early 17th century on the site of an earlier Anglo-Saxon cross. Debenham is no fossil from times past, however. It has several fine modern buildings among the old and remains a thriving community.

8. Turn right out of the teashop and continue along the lane out of the village. Pass Maltings farmhouse on the left and carry on along the lane for a further 160 yards, as far as the end of the first field on the left after Maltings.

9. Turn left up the right hand side of the field. At the time of writing, this path is unsigned but clear on the ground. At the top of the field follow the path and field boundary round to the left. After a couple of zigzags follow the path through a gap in the hedge and on across another field to a road.

10. Turn right for about ¼ mile, ignoring a path on the left after 160 yards.

11. Turn left on a signed path along a track. At a T-junction with a track turn left and follow this back to the start, following the main track round to the right after 35 yards.

Walk 10
GILLINGHAM and BECCLES

If you enjoy riverside walking, this route should be on your 'must do' list! Near the ancient river port of Beccles, the river Waveney sweeps round in an arc. Most of this easy walk is along the banks of the river, calling in near Beccles Quay for tea. After a refreshing break the route continues by the river before cutting inland back to the start. Once an important commercial route, today the river is busy with pleasure craft so there is always something interesting to watch as you follow the paths described.

The Quay at Beccles Quay is in an enviable position overlooking the river and has plenty of tables outside to enjoy the activity. It is open every day throughout the year between 9 am and 5 pm, perhaps closing earlier in winter, serving a good selection of cakes, pastries and generous sandwiches. Telephone: 01502 713147.

DISTANCE: 4½ miles.

MAP: OS Outdoor Leisure 40 The Broads.

STARTING POINT: Gillingham village hall (GR 412917).

HOW TO GET THERE: Gillingham is signed from the A146 Norwich-Beccles road about 1 mile north-west of Beccles. The village hall is on the left. There is no public car park in the village but there are several spots where it is possible to leave a car without causing inconvenience.

ALTERNATIVE STARTING POINT: If you want to visit the teashop at the beginning or end of your walk, start at Beccles Quay where there is a public car park. To find the teashop, walk along the road towards Beccles, to the left of the Loaves and Fishes. Continue ahead at a crossroads, along Northgate. You will then start the walk at point 4.

THE WALK

1. Walk along the road almost opposite the village hall, called The Street. After 100 yards take the first road on the left, called Kings Dam. Continue along this quiet lane for about ½ mile, round two zigzag bends.

2. About 60 yards after a house called Dunburgh Wood turn left along a signed path which drops quite steeply. At the bottom, when the fence on the left ends, turn left. The path soon reaches the river bank.

The Waveney is the most southerly of the main Broads rivers and is the boundary between Norfolk and Suffolk. In the past the river was an important transport route with barges pulled by horses on towpaths along the river banks as well as sailing wherries.

☕ **3.** Continue along the river bank for 1½ miles to a road bridge over the river. Turn right over the bridge, then take the first left, Fen Lane, to Beccles Quay and the teashop.

Beccles presents a superb townscape when approached along the river with mellow brick houses rising above the flat Gillingham Marshes on the steep eastern bank of the Waveney. Dominating all is the tower of St Michael's, detached from the main body of the church. Its ten bells are highly regarded by campanologists. In the days when wherries sailed the Waveney, Beccles was a thriving river port and the working ships tied up at the staithes or quays, now the haunt of pleasure craft. Narrow streets called scores lead up into the town, quite a climb!

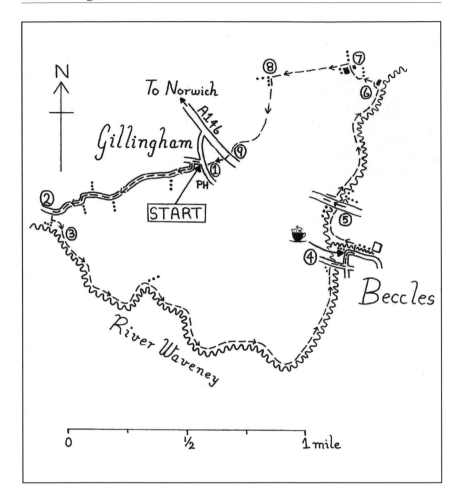

N
↑

To Norwich

Gillingham

START

PH

River Waveney

Beccles

0   ½   1 mile

4. Cross a footbridge over a branch of the river a few yards to the right and turn left. Follow the path round to the bypass.

5. Go under the bridge and immediately turn right up on to the bypass. Turn right. About 50 yards after the bridge take a track on the right which leads back to the river. Turn left to continue walking along the river bank.

6. When the path by the river ends near a house, cross a stile by a metal field gate and follow the path for a short distance up the right-hand side of a field to a second stile. Cross this and turn left along a

The river Waveney.

track which is soon surfaced with concrete. Follow the track between farm buildings.

7. Immediately after leaving the farm turn left along a similarly surfaced track. When this shortly bends left back into the farm, continue in the same direction along an unsurfaced track for about 600 yards.

8. Turn left on a waymarked path to walk with the hedge on the right and follow it to a main road.

9. Cross the road and continue in the same direction on a path which soon leads back to Gillingham village hall.

Walk 11
THE BATH HILLS and BUNGAY

The Bath Hills near Bungay were known to the Romans who grew vines on their favoured south-facing slopes. As hills go, they are not high and the gentle climb is well worth the effort for the views across the plain of the river Waveney. Delightful at any season, this is perhaps a walk at its best in winter when the panoramas are less hidden by leaves. In summer they are no more than tantalising glimpses. After following the clear and well-made path along the hills, the route drops down to the ancient town of Bungay which has several interesting historical sites and a splendid teashop. The return leg is an easy stroll by a branch of the river Waveney back to the start in Earsham.

Earsham Street Café is far more than a traditional teashop and has been listed as one of *The Times* Top Ten Tearooms. It is housed in a 17th century building with a colourful past, having been an inn with a cock fighting pit, a bookmakers, a bazaar and now a teashop. There are many tempting suggestions for lunch from a daily specials board that changes with the seasons so a good plan is to time this walk to take advantage of that. Sandwiches and soup are available for a lighter lunch. The teatime traditions are not neglected, however, and the menu features scones, muffins and crumpets as well as a selection of delicious cakes and cream teas. As well as the modern, sophisticated, interior there is a charming, sheltered patio at the rear. It is hard to believe that this delightful sunny area was once a cock fighting pit. The café is open every day betweem 10 am and 4 pm. Telephone 01986 893103. Website: www.humblecake.co.uk

When the teashop is closed, there are many pubs and other eating establishments in Bungay.

DISTANCE: 5 miles.
MAP: OS Outdoor Leisure 40 The Broads.
STARTING POINT: Parking area in Earsham (GR 323891).
HOW TO GET THERE: From the A143 1 mile west of Bungay take a minor road signed 'Earsham'. Opposite the Queen's Head turn right down Milestone Lane to the entrance to a small parking area.
ALTERNATIVE STARTING POINT: If you want to visit the teashop at the beginning or end of your walk, start in Bungay where there is ample parking in Priory Lane car park. To find the teashop, walk into Bungay centre and turn left along Earsham Street, just past the Buttercross. You will then start the walk at point 8.

THE WALK

Note the village sign. It shows Earsham Mill, mentioned in the Domesday Book, as it was in 1793. The tranquil community of Earsham has been involved in conflicts ancient and modern. It is recorded that Vikings sailed up the Waveney to attack the village and in more recent times it had an important role during the Second World War. There were 8 airfields within 12 miles of the village and next to the railway - now closed - was an area used as a marshalling yard for bombs and fuel for the US Airforce.

1. Cross The Street and walk down Station Road opposite. The road is blocked off at the end but a footpath to the left leads onto the bypass. Cross this and walk along Hall Road opposite for 200 yards.

2. Turn right on a little lane called Bath Hills Road. Continue along this for about a mile, passing some flooded gravel pits.

3. After Valley Farm, continue in the same direction along a track.

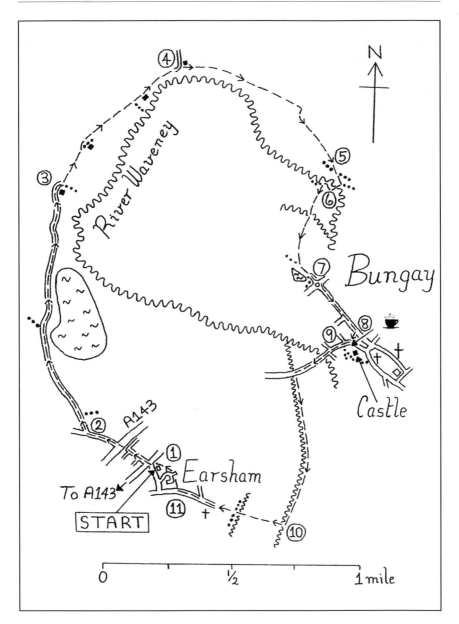

N

River Waveney

④

③

⑤

⑥

⑦ Bungay

⑧

⑨

Castle

A143

②

①
Earsham

To A143

⑪ †

⑩

START

0   ½   1 mile

Some 50 yards after a gate across the track bear left off the track, following the signed path. The path soon becomes a track once more and then starts to climb.

The slopes of these hills face south and have been used for growing vines in both Roman and Norman times. Records show that the Bigod family, who held Bungay Castle, had extensive vineyards here in 1240. The name Bath Hills comes from Bungay's brief flowering as a spa town when a cold spring near Bath House was promoted as health giving in the 1730s.

4. As the track bends sharply left by a bungalow, bear right on a path to continue in the same direction. Follow this delightful path along the hillside until it eventually loses height and comes to a gate.

5. Continue in the same direction, crossing a surfaced drive, to a small wooden gate into a wood. After about 30 yards the path comes to a T-junction. Turn right and follow the path crossing two footbridges.

6. Turn right along the river bank for 85 yards then turn left across a meadow to a gate by a metal gate. (In fact, this is straight ahead from the end of the bridge but the right of way is as described.) Continue on what is now a clear track across the next field, bearing left to a footbridge over the Old River, and on to a stile by a gate. Over the stile, continue along the track to a T-junction by a small lake. Turn left to reach a gate onto a road.

The works across the road is the home of Richard Clay and Son, better known as The Chaucer Press. Bungay has a long tradition of printing, an industry which started at the end of the 18th century. The first edition of 'Alice in Wonderland' was printed in the town.

7. Continue in the same direction into Bungay, going over a roundabout at the bypass. Opposite Barclays Bank turn right on a short path between buildings to emerge almost opposite the teashop.

8. On leaving the teashop turn left. After 85 yards a path on the left leads to the castle, bearing left in front of some garages. If you want to explore the rest of Bungay, continue past the castle into the centre of the town and then retrace your steps.

Bungay Castle is open to the public (free) between 10 am and 4 pm. The ruins we see today are explained by an information board. The Bigod family received enormous estates from William the Conqueror and the first castle on this site dates from that time. Eventually, the Bigods fell out with the Crown (see walk 17) and Henry II ordered Hugh Bigod to dismantle his keep. A siege was set. The usual way of destroying castles was by undermining - cavities were excavated in the walls, supported by wood props which were then set alight causing the walls to collapse. Hugh paid a fine instead and the castle was spared but a mine gallery can still be seen. Hugh died two years later, ironically while fighting for the king in Syria. Most of the castle we see today was built by another Bigod, Roger, in about 1294. When the last Earl Bigod died in 1307 the castle passed to the Crown and was used as a source of building stone as it fell into disuse.

Bungay is an interesting and attractive town which repays exploration. Its curious name possibly derives from bongue meaning a good ford and it was certainly an important crossing point on the Waveney for the Romans. It was a prosperous river port, able to rebuild after a disastrous fire swept through the town in 1688. Opposite the west end of St Mary's church is one of the few buildings to survive, with three oriel windows and carved sills above the modern shopfront. The centre is dominated by ecclesiastical buildings with two churches within 200 yards of each other. Until the Dissolution there was a nunnery in Bungay and St Mary's was its church. St Mary's is now surplus to requirements and is cared for by the Churches Conservation Trust. Behind it and the ruins of the convent is the much older Holy Trinity with a round tower dating back to AD 1000 and some splendid gargoyles.

9. Continue along the road. Some 250 yards after the last house, immediately before a second bridge over the river, turn left along a track and follow it by the river to a footbridge across it.

10. Cross the bridge and follow the clear path opposite which eventually becomes a lane leading into Earsham, passing the church which is usually locked.

Earsham is an ancient settlement. The church possibly stands on the site of a Roman camp and evidence of Saxon burials has been found in the field opposite.

11. About 200 yards after the church, turn right on a path between cottages. This soon leads through a small estate of new houses, back to the start.

Walk 12
BURGATE and WORTHAM

The countryside south-west of Diss is very attractive - gently rolling and well supplied with mature trees, picture postcard thatched cottages and pretty ponds complete with bullrushes. The route also passes land owned by Howard Nurseries, one of the largest suppliers of perennials for the garden, giving some exceptionally attractive, flower-filled fields in season. This undemanding short circuit makes an enjoyable afternoon's expedition, calling in at Wortham for tea.

Wortham Tea Shop is outstanding and deservedly popular, recognised by having won the *East Anglian Times* Best Teashop in Suffolk competition. It is housed is in a converted Elizabethan hay barn next to the village post office. It has some tables outside in an attractive tea garden. Wortham is an unusually spacious village with extensive commons and the teashop overlooks these. Cream teas with a choice of speciality jams are served together with cakes and other teatime goodies. For lunch there is a wide choice. Tasty soup is very welcome on a winter walk and there are jacket potatoes with various fillings and a range of sandwiches or ploughman's for a snack. Full meals, with a special children's menu, are also served. It is open between 9 am and 5 pm all year, closing at 4 pm at the weekend. Telephone: 01379 783210. Website: www.worthamteashop.co.uk

DISTANCE: 3½ miles.

MAP: OS Explorer 230 Diss & Harlestone.

STARTING POINT: St Mary's church, Burgate (GR 083755).

HOW TO GET THERE: From the A143 at Wortham take a minor road signed 'Mellis 2 Yaxley 4 Burgate'. After a mile turn right, signed 'Burgate 1 Gislingham 3'. Park on the wide verge by the church or, if this is full, on a triangle at a sharp bend 300 yards north of the church.

ALTERNATIVE STARTING POINT: If you want to visit the teashop at the beginning or end of your walk, start in Wortham where there are some parking places on the common near the teashop. You will then start the walk at point 6.

THE WALK

On Christmas Day AD 856 a young man called Edmund, aged just 15, was crowned King of East Anglia at Bures. At that time the Vikings were constantly threatening the country, pillaging, murdering and raping. Young King Edmund took up arms against the marauding invaders but was defeated. When he refused to give up his Christian faith he was executed by being bound to a tree and used as target practice by the Viking archers. His saintly nature was soon revealed, however, as his corpse did not decay and his beard and nails continued to grow. These provided saleable relics for the monks who tended his shrine which soon became a place of pilgrimage. It was renamed St Edmondsbury and is now called Bury St Edmunds. The name of this small hamlet – Burgate – is supposed to come from a Saxon word, burgan for burial, and a Danish word, gate meaning road and this is supposed to refer to the route the burial procession took as it conveyed the body of the king and martyr to its final resting place. As things turned out, it was less final than was thought! The body was apparently abducted to Toulouse in the Middle Ages and then returned to England – minus its head – at the start of the 20th century and now rests in Arundel Castle.

There may well have been a church on this site since Saxon times. The present building was erected in the 14th century and contains one of Suffolk's foremost brasses, that of Sir William Burgate, who died in 1409, and his wife Elenora. The church is often locked but the key is available nearby and more information can be found inside.

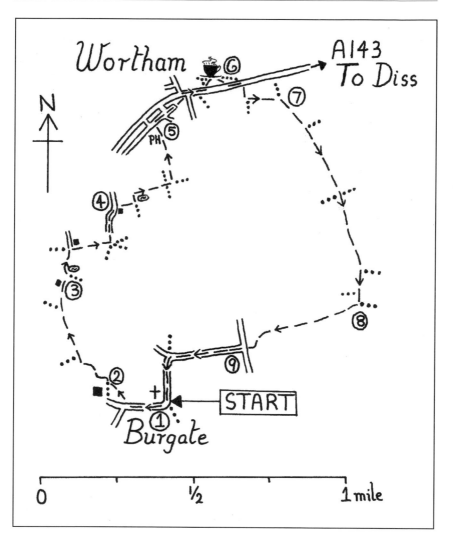

1. With your back to the church turn right along the lane. When it bends left at the entrance to Hall Farm, turn right on a signed path and follow it half left across a field to a track.

2. Turn right. When the track forks, bear right to walk along the right-hand edge of a wood. When the wood on the left ends, continue ahead on the right-hand side of a field to the right of a corrugated iron shed. Walk up a short grassy path to a track.

3. Turn left. When the track becomes a surfaced lane, by a chocolate box thatched cottage, turn right along a track. After 250 yards turn left along a crosstrack which soon becomes a surfaced lane.

4. Immediately after a building on the right, once a chapel, turn right along a signed path on the left-hand side of a field to a cross track. Turn left for 40 yards then right on an initially hedged path, passing a pond on the right. Cross a track and continue into the next field for 10 yards then turn left on a path indicated by a fingerpost. This emerges in the car park of the Dolphin Inn.

5. Cross the car park to a road and turn right to the teashop, easily spotted by its teapot sign.

Wortham is a very spread out village with houses around the extensive greens and commons. The church is over a mile away, suggesting perhaps that the village, like many others, has moved during its long history. Note the unusually magnificent entrance to the primary school, passed on your right.

6. From the teashop turn left along the main road for 100 yards. Take a signed path on the right to a wooden bridge over a ditch. Head left to the far end of the field to a gap in the hedge onto a track.

7. Turn right and walk along the track for ¾ mile, ignoring all side paths.

8. At a T-junction with a crosstrack turn right and follow it to a road.

9. Cross the road and carry on in the same direction along a lane, following it round to the left, back to the start.

Walk 13
WALBERSWICK

*M*uch *of this exceptionally interesting short walk explores Walberswick National Nature Reserve. This is a mosaic of different habitats including heath, sand dunes and salt marsh so the entire route has many features of ecological interest. Bird watchers will particularly enjoy the marshes which are home to marsh harriers, bearded tits and the bitterns that can sometimes be heard booming across the reedbeds.*

The Parish Lantern is an attractive tearoom beside the gift shop and has a sheltered and popular patio behind. The name refers to the moon (Walberswick has no street lighting) and the building is Georgian and, in its time, has been a corn-merchant's house and the village school. They serve a good range of cakes. Other teatime goodies include cookies, shortbread, crumpets and toasted teacakes, not forgetting cream teas. Equally tempting on a hot day is the choice of local ices including raspberry, summer pudding and rhubarb. For lunch there is a choice of sanwiches, which includes locally caught crab when available. Alternatively, these fillings can be served with a jacket potato. The Parish Lantern is open every day from March to December from 10 am until 5 pm (later in the summer). In January and February they open on Friday, Saturday and Sunday and during half term. Telephone 01502 723173.

When the teashop is closed there are alternative sources of refreshment in the village, including the Bell, which serves food.

DISTANCE: 3 miles.

MAP: OS Explorer 231 Southwold & Bungay.

STARTING POINT: Ferry Road car park, Walberswick (GR 500749).

HOW TO GET THERE: From the A12 take the B1387, signed 'Walberswick 4'. Follow this to the village and continue right through it to the Ferry Road car park at the far end, by the river.

ALTERNATIVE STARTING POINT: The teashop is close to the end of the walk. If you wish to visit it at the start, use the car park on the right on the way into the village: the access road is almost opposite the teashop. You will then start the route at point 10.

THE WALK

Walberswick is an attractive village which has been a thriving port in the Middle Ages and a haunt of artists in the 19th century, and is now a popular tourist destination. In the Tate Gallery are three Walberswick paintings by Philip Wilson Steer who spent several summers here from 1884 onwards. At the outbreak of the First World War the Scottish art nouveau architect Charles Rennie Mackintosh lived in Walberswick and for a while was suspected of being a German spy, partly due to his habit of taking evening walks with his wife!

1. Walk down to the quay and turn left. Continue along a bank with the river Blyth on your right as far as a bridge over the river.

As with most rivers in East Anglia, the Blyth was an important shipping route at one time and Walberswick was a flourishing port. Much trading took place with Iceland and some Icelanders settled in the village. Trade fell away in the late 15th century when vessels too large to navigate the somewhat narrow river came into use.

2. At the bridge turn left away from the river on a broad track.

3. Watch out for seats on the left and right. Do not take a path on the

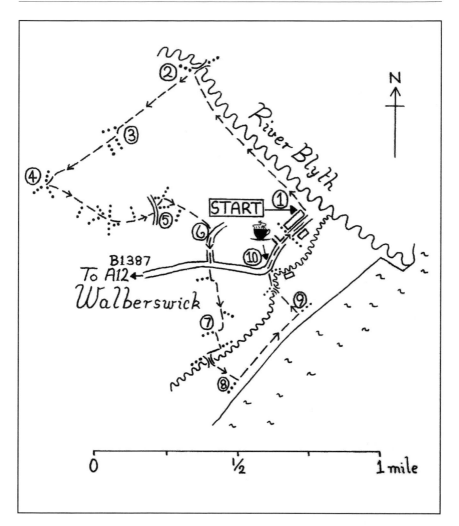

right here but continue along the surfaced path for another 40 yards to a second path on the right. Follow this ignoring a path on the left.

4. When the path approaches a fence with a gate next to a notice board, turn sharp left, almost back on yourself. When the path reaches an open area ignore the first bridleway on the left and continue for 20 yards to a second, on a right hand bend. Take this to continue in more or less the same direction to very soon reach a track. Turn left to press on in the same direction to a lane.

Walberswick National Nature Reserve covers 700 hectares and is exceptionally diverse, containing large reedbeds, visited later, dunes, shingle and saltings as well as heath and woodland. The reserve was declared in 1972 and is partly owned by English Nature and partly managed by them under agreement from the landowner. Over 100 species of birds have been recorded as nesting here and anything may turn up at times of migration. Regular breeding species include avocet, bittern, marsh harrier and bearded reedling while winter visitors include hen harriers and the rough legged buzzard. The reserve is also important for several rare insects. This variety in habitat is only maintained by active management including reedcutting, scrub clearance and water control.

5. Turn left. After 30 yards fork right on the second of two parallel tracks for 50 yards then turn right on a clear path. Follow this to a lane.

To the right along the road is the church which illustrates the changing fortunes of Walberswick. Built in 1493, it was once as imposing as many other churches in this area, such as those at Blythburgh and Southwold. As the port declined, the parish became too poor to maintain it and pulled part of it down in 1695, leaving the ruins we see today.

6. Turn right to a main road. Cross the road and take a signed path opposite. Follow this round the left-hand perimeter of a large field.

7. Just after turning the corner at the far end of the field, turn left on a path through a gap in the hedge and continue on a boardwalk across the marsh. When the boardwalk finishes at a bank turn right along the river to a footbridge. Cross this and follow the path ahead to a shingle bank.

8. Climb onto the bank and turn left. Walk along the bank or beach and look out for the first of the beach huts.

9. Just before the first beach hut, bear left to cross a footbridge to a track. Turn right to a road and right again to the teashop on the left, beside the village green.

10. Turn left out of the teashop through the village back to the start.

Walk 14
THORPENESS

This delightful walk on heath and shore visits the sites of dreams and fantasies. The route starts by Sizewell nuclear power station which was built when it was still thought that nuclear power could give unlimited cheap, clean power. It soon leaves this behind and wends its way across heathland to a unique purpose-built holiday village, the realisation of one man's dream. After tea, it returns by the sea along and below low cliffs. There are many attractive spots to linger and this part of the route is of outstanding botanical interest.

The Meare Tearoom in Thorpeness enjoys a superb position overlooking the lake so you can be entertained by the antics of the swans and boaters and admire the view of the Cloud House poking above the trees. They serve an excellent selection of cakes, some of which are gluten free, as well as cream teas with clotted cream. For lunch there is a choice of sandwiches or filled jacket potatoes and, most notably, an outstanding range of home-made quiche. They are open every day from 9.30 am throughout the year. Telephone: 01728 452156. Website: www.meareshop.co.uk.

DISTANCE: 5 miles.
MAP: OS Explorer 212 Woodbridge & Saxmundham.
STARTING POINT: Sizewell beach car park (GR 474629).
HOW TO GET THERE: From the A12 take the B1122 or B1119 to Leiston and follow the signs to Sizewell Beach. Continue along the road until it ends at the beach car park.
ALTERNATIVE STARTING POINT: If you want to visit the teashop at the beginning or end of your walk, start in Thorpeness where there is a public car park next to the teashop. You will then start the walk at point 7.

THE WALK
Three nuclear power stations were originally planned for this site. Sizewell A was built in the early 1960s and first fed power into the National Grid in 1966. When the time came to build Sizewell B, 20 years later, there was enormous and wide ranging opposition which led to a public enquiry. This started in January 1983 and lasted for two years, cost ⁴20m and heard from 200 expert witnesses. The final report found in favour of building the power station, concluding that any risk and the undoubted damage to the landscape are acceptable in the national economic interest. It is most unlikely that Sizewell C will ever be built. Privatisation of the electricity industry revealed that the supposed economic advantages of nuclear power were always extremely dubious.

1. Leave the car park along the road and take the first road on the left, signed 'Sizewell Hall'.

In the 18th century Sizewell village was a notorious centre for smuggling. A record 8,000 gallons of gin were apparently once landed in a single night.

2. After the last of the farm buildings on the right, by an attractive thatched cottage, turn right along a track. Walk along the track for ½ mile, ignoring a bridleway on the left, to a complex junction of tracks and paths.

3. Pass a track on the left and continue for 20 yards to a crosstrack which soon joins with the first track on the left. Leave the track at this point and continue in the same direction on a signed grassy path.

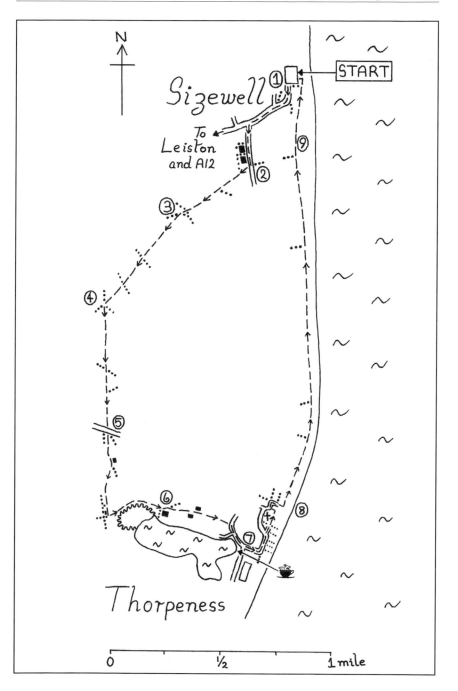

N

Sizewell

START ①

To
Leiston
and A12

②

③

④

⑤

⑥

⑦

⑧

⑨

Thorpeness

0   ½   1 mile

Keep on this path alongside a field, soon walking between low wire fences, ignoring all side and crosspaths.

Walking along this path it is interesting to contrast the vegetation on either side. On the left nature is being allowed to take its course with the result that bracken and silver birch are the dominant plants and, if left alone for long enough, a wood will eventually develop. On the right the fields are planted with crops. At the time of writing this is flax and the blue blossom seems to reflect the sky.

4. Just after the field on the right ends, turn left through a metal gate on a crosspath. Ignore a path bearing left and go ahead to a gate. Go over a cross path and maintain direction to join a track. Again, continue in the same direction to a road.

5. Cross the road and take a track opposite, ignoring a track on the left onto a golf course, to a barn. Go to the right of the barn for 40 yards then, as the main path bears left, continue straight on along a grassy path. At a crosspath bear left, passing a house, and then turn left on a path marked with a yellow arrow, soon walking between the edge of the golf course and a branch of the lake in Thorpeness, The Meare.

This is an artificial lake. In 1903 Mr Glencairn Stuart Ogilvie inherited his family estate. In 1910 there was extensive flooding and when Mr Ogilvie came to see it he was so impressed he is reported as saying, 'Let's keep it, and build a holiday village around it.' Perhaps this story is apocryphal but certainly in 1910 work began on a planned holiday village with the digging out of the lake. It is only 3 feet deep and was envisaged as a children's paradise - youngsters could rent an island for the day.

☕ **6.** At the drive to the golf course turn left for 20 yards then right on a track, soon passing between the House in the Clouds and a windmill. At a T-junction with a road, turn right to the teashop.

Thorpeness windmill started life 2 miles away at Aldringham where it was used for grinding corn. In the winter of 1922/3 it was dismantled and rebuilt here and converted to pump water. Originally water for Thorpeness was brought up from a well by a metal wind pump but it was thought that this was something of a blot on the landscape and so this building was imported to add old world charm to the business of moving water. The water was stored in an iron water tank supported on a steel frame, another structure deemed inappropriate so this was made into a hybrid house-cum-water tower – the famous House in the Clouds. After the war the windmill fell into disuse and decay. It was restored in 1976/7 and is now undergoing further restoration at the time of writing.

7. Turn right out of the teashop to a road. Turn left then first right, signed 'Country Club' and turn left at the end. Turn right immediately after Drake House and, at the end of the surfaced road, continue in the same direction, passing the church on the left. Follow the track round to the left, then turn right along a road. Carry on along this as it bends right and then continue in the same direction on a path to the shore.

Thorpeness is unique. It was conceived as a planned holiday village providing for self-catering family holidays. The houses were intended to be all let on leases of not less than a month. Everything was provided except linen and plate and the rents were high so it was very much a middle class holiday resort. The houses and other facilities were mainly built between 1911 and 1937 and are mostly of heavily disguised concrete. Some houses have been built later which were not part of the original plan and the concept of a fantasy holiday village with no attraction to day trippers has become blurred as properties have been sold off. People now live here all the year round, some being those who have fond memories of happy holidays here as children.

8. Turn left along the shore. At first it is quite hard going along the shingle but a path soon develops at the bottom of the low cliffs. This eventually climbs onto the top of the cliffs and is easy to follow.

Shingle is the most difficult habitat for plants to colonise. It is unstable as the pebbles roll about in a storm, crushing the plants. Water drains rapidly through the large spaces between the stones so even in a damp climate the plants can be short of water. As the water runs away it carries with it the small supply of nutrients and, to make things worse, the plants are exposed to high levels of damaging salt. Despite this, a few hardy species are adapted to survive in these difficult conditions. The most attractive is the yellow horned poppy. It has thick, almost succulent, grey-blue leaves and large yellow flowers which produce long, curved pods containing thousands and thousands of tiny black seeds.

9. After a couple of miles the path drops down off the clifftop at the far end of a caravan site and threads its way through low dunes towards a low building (public conveniences) and then bears left, back to the start.

Walk 15
TUNSTALL FOREST and SNAPE MALTINGS

The focus of this easy walk is the world famous complex at Snape Maltings, centred round the concert hall, said to be among the best in Europe. The route starts and finishes by the river Alde but much of it is on clear paths in Tunstall Forest and over Blaxhall Heath. The latter is a remnant of the lowland heath, known as sandlings, which once covered much of this part of Suffolk. It is glorious in late summer when the heather is in bloom.

The Granary Tea Shop is to be found in one of the Maltings buildings and it also has tables outside. It serves a wide selection of interesting cakes as well as light meals such as quiche, pasties and filled rolls. The walls of the attractive interior are decorated with paintings for sale. It is open throughout the year from 10 am until 5 pm, 5.30 pm at weekends. Telephone: 01728 688303. Website: www.snapemaltings.co.uk

DISTANCE: 5½ miles.

MAP: OS Explorer 212 Woodbridge & Saxmundham.

STARTING POINT: Iken Cliff picnic site and car park (GR 399563).

HOW TO GET THERE: From the A12 near Woodbridge take the A1152 and follow it until it ends at a roundabout near RAF Bentwaters. Continue in the same direction on the B1069, through Tunstall and following the signs for Snape. After about 1¼ miles turn right on a minor road signed 'Iken 2½ Sudbourne 3'. Some 400 yards after a crossroads turn left on a track to Iken Cliff picnic site and car park. Approaching from the north, take the A1094 towards Aldeburgh from the A12 north of Stratford St Andrew. After 1½ miles turn right on the B1069 and follow this through the village of Snape and past Snape Maltings. Soon after passing the Maltings, bear left on a minor road signed 'Iken 2 Orford 5¼'. After a mile turn left, signed 'Iken 2', for 400 yards then turn left on a track to Iken Cliff picnic site and car park.

ALTERNATIVE STARTING POINT: If you want to visit the teashop at the beginning or end of your walk, start at Snape Maltings where there is ample parking. You will then begin the walk at point 13.

THE WALK

The river Alde was a busy shipping route until the latter half of the 19th century and coal, corn and other commodities were moved through the dock here at Iken Cliff. In more recent times this attractive spot has become a popular picnic site, now owned by Suffolk County Council.

1. From the bottom right-hand corner of the picnic site take a path on the right. At a complex junction of paths by two houses bear slightly right on a gently rising path and follow this to a lane.

Away to the left, rising above the muddy tidal flats of the river, the remote and ancient church, St Botolph's, can be seen. There was a monastic cell there as early as AD 647 and the chancel contains a Saxon cross carved with dragons. Sadly, the nave was almost destroyed by fire in 1968.

2. Turn right. After 100 yards turn left on a signed path.The right of way nominally lies over a stile and along the right hand side of a field. However, the stile is unusable and on the ground the path now lies on the right hand side of the fence. Follow the fence round to the left to join a surfaced track for about 100 yards.

3. Turn right again immediately to pass to the right of a barn so that initially you are walking back almost in the same direction but on the

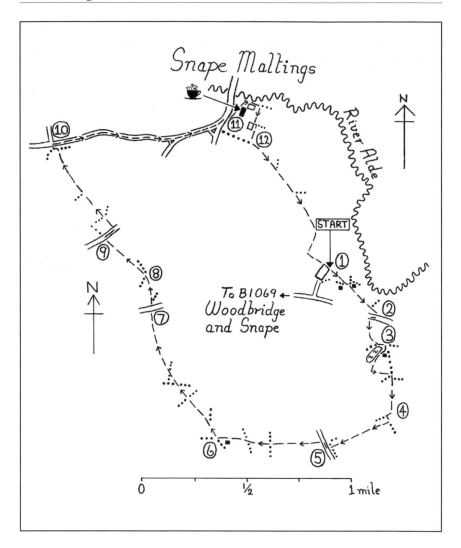

opposite side of a large pond. At the top right-hand corner of the field turn left to walk along the top edge of the field with a wood on the right. When the wood ends at a crosspath, turn right to continue walking with the wood on the right.

4. After about 300 yards turn right on a signed path and left after 40 yards. After another 40 yards turn right to walk along the right-hand side of a field, with a strip of wood on the right, to a lane.

5. Cross the lane and go right for a few yards to a track on the left into Tunstall Forest. Continue walking along this track as far as a house on the left, ignoring all side tracks.

6. Just after the house, turn right on a track. After 150 yards, as the track bears right, bear left on a grassy path. Continue ahead at a broad crosstrack then bear left at a fork 100 yards after this.

Tunstall Forest together with Rendlesham and Dunwich Forests make up the 14 square miles of Aldewood Forest. The area was planted with conifers by the Forestry Commission in the 1920s. Prior to this, the area had been heathland with little agricultural potential. During the First World War there had been a shortage of timber for trenches and, consequently, the Forestry Commission was set up in 1919 to create a strategic reserve of timber. Almost all of their planting was conifers because these are very quick growing in the warm(!), wet British climate and the areas chosen were poor quality farmland, such as this.

7. Cross a lane and continue in the same direction.

8. After about 300 yards the path splits into three. Follow the middle branch, soon passing a plaque on a stone pillar, to a road.

9. Turn right along the road for 100 yards then turn left. Follow the path ahead, ignoring all side turns, to a lane.

☕ **10.** Turn right along the lane. At a junction with a main road turn left to Snape Maltings and the teashop.

In the summer of 1941 a young English composer called Benjamin Britten from Suffolk, living in the United States, came across the work of the poet George Crabbe. As a parish priest in the late 18th century, Crabbe led an unremarkable life in Aldeburgh but in his verses he told the grim truth about rural conditions at that time, unlike his Romantic contemporaries. Talking about almshouses:

> You Have placed your poor, your pitiable few
> There, in one house, throughout their lives to be
> The pauper palace which they have to see:
> It is a prison with a milder name
> Which few inhabit without dread or shame.

This discovery was a defining point in Britten's life and he realised that he would find his best inspiration back in Suffolk. He returned home and began work on the opera 'Peter Grimes', inspired by the work of Crabbe. Its first performance in 1945, with Britten's friend and companion Peter Pears in the title role, marked the reopening of Sadlers Wells Theatre after the war and the start of his brilliant career as a composer of opera.

In 1947 Britten, Pears and the librettist Eric Crozier decided to start a small music festival at Aldeburgh to give British opera a better stage in its home country. Early events were held in halls and churches in Aldeburgh and the surrounding area. As the festival's popularity and fame grew it became apparent that a large and permanent concert hall was needed.

Snape Maltings is a 19th-century industrial complex built by Newson Garrett, one of a family who were leading industrialists and intellectuals of their day. One daughter was Elizabeth Garrett Anderson, who was both the first woman doctor and the first woman mayor, taking office as mayor of Aldeburgh in 1908. Another was Dame Millicent Garrett Fawcett, a suffragette and one of the founders of Newnham College, Cambridge. The brick buildings were originally used to prepare local barley for brewing and the malt produced was shipped out down the Alde. It was opened as a concert hall in 1967 but suffered a major setback when it was gutted by fire on the first night of the festival in 1969. Brilliantly restored in a year, it is widely regarded as among the finest in Europe, thanks to its magnificent acoustics. As well as the concert hall, the complex contains teaching rooms, shops, restaurants and bars surrounded by lawns with statues by Barbara Hepworth.

11. After tea turn right to walk by the river. The path soon comes to a notice saying that it is impassable at high tide. This is true and is optimistic at low tide unless you are unusually partial to mud. Some 70 yards after the notice turn right. Follow the path past the end of the overflow car park.

12. Turn left at a T-junction and follow the clear path across field and marsh back to the start, ignoring paths on the left.

Walk 16
DUNWICH

This walk is packed with interest, both human and natural. It explores part of Dunwich Forest before skirting the historic and atmospheric village. It is easy to divert a little way off the route to explore it further and perhaps visit the fascinating museum. The route then leads by lanes, woods and heathland to the National Trust Visitor Centre at Dunwich Heath, which has a brilliantly positioned tea room on the cliffs. After tea comes the climax of this walk, the traverse of Dunwich Heath. Do try to make at least one visit in high summer when the heath is a sea of brilliant mauve and purple – a stunning sight. The path climbs gently to an excellent viewpoint before more woodland walking leads back to the start. It is particularly interesting to see how different regimes of land management have led to different vegetation within a short distance and to see the National Trust's efforts to replace one with another.

 Coastguard Tearoom at the National Trust Visitor Centre at Dunwich Heath offers excellent fare including a delicious selection of cakes and cream teas with clotted cream. For lunch there is a choice of soup, filled jacket potatoes and pasties supplemented by daily specials such as potato skins with cheese, bacon and mushrooms. There is some accommodation inside for less clement weather but most of the tables are outside to take advantage of the superb position on the cliffs. Don't delay too long to enjoy a visit: we are told that in 60 years it will have joined Dunwich beneath the waves! Webite: www.nationaltrust.org.uk/dunwich-heath-and-beach

DISTANCE: 5 miles.

MAPS: OS Explorer 231 Southwold and Bungay.

STARTING POINT: Forestry Commission car park and picnic site at Dunwich Forest (GR 466709).

HOW TO GET THERE: From the B1125, Blythburgh Westleton road, 1¾ miles south of Blythburgh and 2½ miles north of Westleton at a cross roads, take a minor road, signed 'Dunwich 2¼' to a car park and picnic site on the left after 1½ miles. Note: there are several other roads signed for Dunwich closer to Westleton; these will not lead you to the starting point. Also, the starting point is the **second** car park (on the left), not the first, which is on the right on the directions given.

ALTERNATIVE STARTING POINT: If you wish to visit the teashop at the beginning or end of your walk, start in at the National Trust Visitor Centre at Dunwich Heath where there is ample parking (charge). The teashop is in the old Coastguard building. You will then start the walk at point 8.

THE WALK

1. Take a path on the right of the car park a few yards after the end of the entrance drive for 80 yards to a metal kissing gate. Through the gate turn right to a crosstrack. Turn right and immediately left to continue in the same direction. After about 250 yards follow the main path round to the left, ignoring an immediate narrow path on the right. Carry on for about 275 yards to a second path on the right.

Dunwich Forest, together with Tunstall and Rendlesham Forests, was planted by the Forestry Commission in the 1920s (see Walk 15, page 73).

2. Turn right for about ¼ mile to eventually reach a gate on the right onto a broad track.

3. Turn right and follow the track to a road, passing the entrance to Bridge Nurseries, which also has a tearoom.

4. Turn left to a church. Turn right. (Continue along the road if you wish to visit Dunwich and its fascinating museum.) At a T-junction turn right and walk along the road for about ¼ mile.

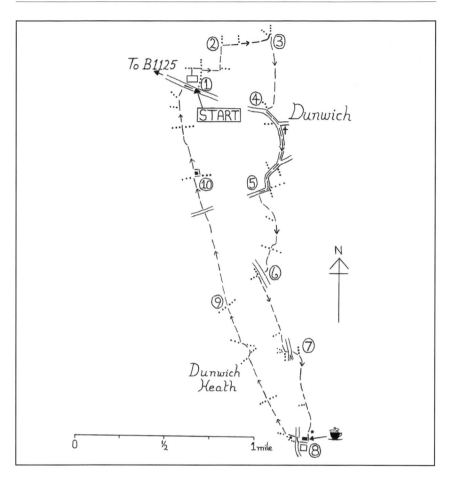

These days, Dunwich is a small, mainly Victorian, village but it has a long history that now lies beneath the waves. The Romans reputedly built a fort here but today the site is a mile or so offshore. The city grew in Saxon times around the sheltered port and expanded rapidly after the Norman Conquest to become one of England's top 10 towns – rich and prosperous, with a huge fleet trading over much of the Continent and Scandinavia. Dunwich's position led to its prosperity but also held the seeds of its downfall. The cliffs that protected it were subject to constant erosion. Defences were erected as the medieval citizens battled the perennial problem but on the 14th January 1328 disaster struck. A huge storm drove the sea against the spit of land called the Kings Holme, shifting the shingle and effectively blocking the entrance to Dunwich harbour. Despite the strenuous efforts of its inhabitants to clear the harbour entrance, ships and revenue began to move along with the

estuary mouth to Walberswick (see Walk 13, page 61) causing much acrimony between the inhabitants of the two towns and a number of deaths. The sea continued to eat away the coast and tales of a lost city under the waves are indeed true. All that remains today are the walls of the leper hospital in the grounds of this relatively modern church and the buttress of one of the last churches to fall into the sea, rebuilt here.

By the middle of the 18th century, the town had been all but abandoned and yet it continued to elect its two members of parliament as one of the rotten boroughs. At the end of the 18th century, people apparently travelled to Dunwich on election day to go out in a boat to the point where the town hall used to be to cast their vote. The freemen also continued to elect magistrates and bailiffs. By the time of the 1832 Reform Act, which abolished rotten boroughs, there were just 8 residents left in the constituency of Dunwich, represented in parliament by two MPs!

5. Some 100 yards after a sharp right-hand bend, turn left along a signed path along a track to the Dairy House. At the end of the track continue ahead on a path through the woods, crossing a track, to emerge on a lane.

6. Cross the lane and immediately turn left to walk on a permissive path parallel with the lane as far as an open area.

☕ **7.** Bear left back to the lane at the start of the one-way system. Cross the lane and follow a path through the gorse and heather to the Coastguard Buildings that house the teashop. It is worth pausing to visit the informative Seawatch observation post.

The cliffs here are made up of soft clays and sands easily eroded by the sea. A steeply sloping shingle beach lies in front of the cliffs. The rounded flint pebbles come from the pebble beds at the top of the cliff. During a storm waves can reach the foot of the cliffs, eroding the sand beds at the base. This undercutting removes the support for the pebble beds above which fall, causing the cliff top to recede. This is why it is very dangerous to venture close to the cliff edge. The largest waves are produced by storms from a northerly direction so that there is movement of shingle southwards; a process called longshore drift. In this way, these cliffs supply much of the shingle for Orford Ness, Felixstowe and other beaches to the south.

8. Turn right out of the teashop to the car park access road at a finger post. Turn right for 50 yards then turn left along a track, passing the field studies barn on your left. Some 20 yards after the barn, at a picnic site, turn right on a rising path. Follow the path across the heath, turning left then right at a major cross path to keep on in much the same direction, as shown by the Suffolk coast and heath path waymark.

This looks like a wild and natural landscape but is actually man-made. Originally this area would have been covered by oak woodland but this was cleared long ago. When the trees were removed, the soil was more exposed to the weather, and nutrients were leached away producing the sandy, acid soil we see today. This is ideal for the heather and other heathland plants that live here today and support many birds and insects. However, traditional use of this ecosystem is not very productive by modern standards and so much of it, along with the plants and animals that make it up, has been lost to more intensive agriculture and forestry, as we saw at the start of this walk. During the Second World War, Dunwich Heath was requisitioned for military training in preparation for D-Day, and anti-aircraft guns were positioned on the cliffs. Some remnants of this can still be seen, such as the rifle butts by the seat at the top of the rise. After the war, it was used for informal camping, which caused further damage. So it was sold to the National Trust, whose aim is essentially to conserve it as heathland. Active management is essential since, left to itself, it would eventually, over hundreds of years, return to oak woodland. Conservation does not consist of letting nature get on with it. A conscious decision has to be made about what is important and then the area has to be actively managed to that end.

9. At the next cross path continue ahead on a track to a road. Cross the road to keep on along the track to reach a T-junction with a bridleway at a farm.

The land bordering the track is Mount Pleasant farm that used to be managed as a modern farm. The National Trust bought it in 2002 and is working with the RSPB to turn it back to acid grassland and heather. Crops will be grown for some years but taken away and no fertiliser added so that the soil becomes depleted of nutrients. Then it will be sown with an appropriate mixture of seeds to produce the desired ecosystem. One of the problems for the wildlife of threatened habitats is that, if the area becomes fragmented, the populations of plants and animals become chopped up into small isolated groups, which cannot easily interbreed. This in turn leads to inbreeding that undermines the genetic stability of the population. Thus an aim of wildlife management is to create corridors that allow the populations to mix and interbreed.

10. Turn right for 30 yards then turn left on a signed path and follow this to a road. Turn right to the car park where this walk started.

Walk 17
ORFORD

Though this is a short and level walk, there is so much of interest to see that you will need to allow plenty of time to really do it justice. The route starts by the lively quay and a walk by the river with a good view of Orford Ness soon leads past the ancient church to the square and teashop. Orford is an ancient town, once at the centre of affairs in East Anglia. The keep of the castle dominates the attractive town square and a visit is an absolute must. The route then heads out past the castle to Chantry Point, on the banks of the River Ore, opposite Havergate Island, famous for its avocets. A brisk walk along the sea defences brings you back to the quay.

Penny's Cafe on Pump Street, Orford, is attached to the village General Store, which has been crowned the best village shop in UK and Ireland. They serve a range of breakfasts, light lunches and afternoon tea, with their own homemade pies, scones, platters and excellent cakes. The menu changes with the seasons depending on what fresh ingredients are available. A selection of coffees and teas are offered and if you find one you like, you can buy some in the shop to take home. There are some tables outside overlooking the pump, where dogs are welcome with their own water and biscuits. Penny's is open every day throughout the year from 8.30 am to 5 pm (4 pm on Sunday) with last orders 15 minutes before closing. Telephone: 01394 450219. Website: www.orfordgeneralstore.com.

DISTANCE: 3 miles

MAP: OS Explorer 212 Woodbridge and Saxmundham

STARTING POINT: Orford Quay where there is ample parking in a large public car park (charge). GR 424496

HOW TO GET THERE: Follow the signs to Orford from the A12 near Woodbridge. Drive through the village towards the quay to the car park on the left.

ALTERNATIVE STARTING POINT: If you want to visit the teashop at the beginning or end of your walk, start at the town square where there is some parking. The teashop is on the right on Pump Street. You will then start the walk at point 4.

THE WALK

Orford rose to prominence when the castle was built and the harbour developed in the 12th century. It became a busy and prosperous town and was granted a market charter in 1256. In those days the spit of shingle that now stretches six miles southwest from Orford Ness ended near the quay and protected the harbour. However, the spit grew and grew, apparently at the rate of 15 or 16 metres a year in the 16th century, and eventually throttled the port. Writing in 1722, Daniel Defoe said, 'Orford is now decayed. The sea daily throws up more land, so it is a sea port no longer.' The enterprising residents turned to other ways of making a living, notably oyster fishing and smuggling. The smugglers were very audacious. There are reports of cargo being landed in broad daylight while the outnumbered Revenue men watched helplessly.

The story of the merman of Orford was first written down in about 1207 but was referring to a time some forty years earlier when the castle was being built. Fishermen caught a naked and very hairy wild man or merman. They took him to the castle but no one could get him to talk, despite hanging him up by the feet and torturing him. In the church he showed no sign of reverence or belief. Eventually, he was allowed into the sea contained by nets but managed to escape. I wonder what the real story behind this is. Perhaps the fact that it is today sometimes re-enacted for the tourist trade gives us a clue; after all visitors were as eager for a spectacle and a good story in the 12th century as in the 21st.

1. Return to the road and turn left. Before reaching the Quay, turn left along a signed grassy path along an embankment. Follow this past the

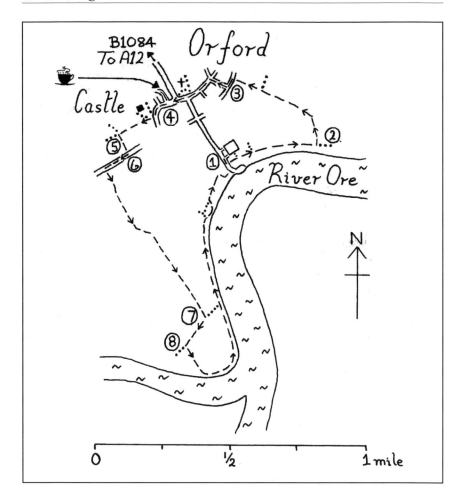

sailing club and along a short hedged section to some steps on the left.

The prominent red and white lighthouse is easy to spot on Orford Ness. In October 1627 there was a great storm and 32 ships were wrecked. This led to the construction of the first lighthouse, though bureaucratic delays meant that 10 years had elapsed before it was finally built. It was a profitable business, taking a toll from all the vessels that sailed past and grants to operate the lighthouse were bought and sold. The structure was replaced several times and the present building dates from 1792. The spit itself has been owned by the military for most of the 20th century. In the First World War it was used for testing parachutes, and in the Second World War for developing radar. It still has many military buildings, including the distinctive 'pagodas' clearly seen on the skyline later in the walk.

2. Go down the steps and follow the path ahead across a field. Immediately after crossing a dyke, turn left to walk with the dyke on the left and follow this path to a lane.

3. Turn left. Take the first lane on the right and then turn left at the next junction. Turn right at the main road then, when this turns right, go ahead into the square. Take a lane on the right to the teashop next to the general store.

The church is essentially Norman, being built just after the castle. It has lost some of its original magnificence. As the wealth of the town declined, the church fell into some disrepair and this was not helped by the attentions of the Puritans in the 17th century who broke up anything they thought smacked of popery. In the 18th century, the eastern end of the nave was walled up and the ruins of the chancel beyond can still be seen. One of the buttresses of the tower gave way in 1830 and much of the tower collapsed, fortunately harming no-one. It was not rebuilt until 1962. The main claim to fame of St Bartholomew's church today is that it was the setting for the first performance of Benjamin Britten's Noye's Fludde in 1958.

4. Return to the square and turn right. Walk out of the square towards the castle. When the road bends sharp left, take a public footpath along the left-hand side of the small castle car park and on past the castle for about 300 yards

The castle was mainly built between 1165 and 1173 by Henry II to control the rebellious local barons, the most prominent of whom was Hugh Bigod, Earl of Norfolk (which in those days meant Suffolk too). He was based at Framlingham and controlled several other castles (see walk 11). Henry II was much troubled by the rebellions of his sons who were supported by the King of France and aided and abetted by Hugh Bigod. The keep was of a revolutionary new design: it is cylindrical inside and polygonal outside, reinforced by three projecting rectangular turrets. This was supposed to make it less liable to collapse if undermined by those besieging it. Inside it is a warren of passages and rooms, including fascinating medieval lavatories. There is a magnificent view of the surrounding countryside from the top. It is now in the care of English Heritage and is open between 10am and 5pm every day from the end of March to the end of October, and weekends in winter. A tour is strongly recommended and there is a very well produced and informative guidebook available.

5. At a cross path turn left along a hedged path to a lane.

6. Turn right along the lane for 200 yards then left along a track, signed 'Footpath'. When the track ends continue ahead along the left hand side of a field. At the end of the field cross a dyke and turn right to walk along the right hand side of a field with the dyke on the right to a gate on to a cross path.

7. Turn right. Cross a bridge and go up onto a bank.

Orford Castle

Standing here a thousand years ago, you would have been facing the open sea. As explained above, the spit grew after the 12th century and the low-lying island opposite formed within its protection. Havergate Island is now an RSPB reserve that may be visited on pre-booked trips (01728 648281). It is famous for the avocet colony that returned there to breed in 1947 after being absent from Britain for 100 years. Avocets are quite unmistakable at close quarters with distinctive black and white plumage and upturned bill. Gulls, terns, shelducks and red shanks are also found on the island.

8. Turn left along the bank and follow the path to Orford Quay. At the quay turn left along a road back to the start.

The quay is now a lively place with fishing boats and pleasure craft There are ferries to Orford Ness now it is in the care of the National Trust (telephone 01728 648024 for details).

Walk 18
DEDHAM and FLATFORD MILL

This walk explores the lovely countryside of Dedham Vale, which inspired the artist John Constable early in the 19th century and still retains its timeless appeal. He said, in a letter written in 1812, 'You know I have always succeeded best with my native scenes. They have charmed me, and I hope they always will.' The whole walk is exceptionally easy, being completely level and on very clear paths. It starts in Dedham, which has many attractive and historic buildings, and makes its way to Flatford Mill, the scene of many of Constable's best known and loved pictures. The return is along the banks of the River Stour and is especially attractive.

Bridge Cottage Tearoom at Flatford is run by the National Trust. There is a well-designed modern building giving indoor accommodation when the weather is less clement, as well as tables in the garden. An excellent selection of delicious cakes and cream teas are served. For lunch there are various platters available and filled jacket potatoes with an unusually wide and interesting selection of fillings. There is a special children's selection and small portions are available. The tea room is open from early March until just before Christmas. In high summer, from the end of May until September, the opening hours are from 10 am until 5.30 pm every day.

Outside this period, it is closed on Monday and Tuesday and it shuts at 3.30 pm in November and December. Telephone: 01206 298260 Website: www.nationaltrust.org.uk/flatford-bridge-cottage

When the tea shop is closed, there are several alternative sources of refreshment in Dedham, most notably the Essex Rose. This is a traditional tea shop serving salads, sandwiches and filled jacket potatoes as well as cakes. It is passed on the route at the junction of Mill Lane and High Street in Dedham, opposite the church (Telephone: 01206 323101).

DISTANCE: 3½ miles

MAP: OS Explorer 196 Sudbury, Hadleigh and Dedham Vale

STARTING POINT: Public car park at Dedham on the B1029 between the town centre and Dedham Mill. (GR 058334)

HOW TO GET THERE: Dedham is on the B1029, signed from the A12.

ALTERNATIVE STARTING POINT: If you want to visit the tea shop at the beginning or end of your walk, start at Flatford Mill, signed from East Bergholt, where there is a public car park (charge). There is a path from the car park to the river and Bridge Cottage. You will then start the walk at point 5.

THE WALK

1. From the car park, return to the road and turn left. At a T junction turn left again.

The River Stour forms the boundary between Suffolk and Essex so Dedham is in Essex whilst Flatford Mill is in Suffolk. Dedham has been settled since Roman times and is mentioned in the Domesday book as having a population of 200. It was a prosperous wool town in the 15th and 16th centuries when the Grammar School was founded: its most famous pupil was John Constable.

Constable is not the only artist to have found inspiration around Dedham. Sir Alfred Munnings, President of the Royal Academy between 1944 and 1949, moved to Castle House on the outskirts of Dedham in 1920. This now houses a collection of his paintings and is open to the public Wednesday to Sunday 2pm to 5pm April to October (Telephone 01206 322127), signed from the centre of Dedham.

2. As the road bends sharp right continue in the same direction along a drive, signed 'Public Footpath Flatford' for 200 yards. When the drive ends bear right on a signed path for 80 yards.

3. Turn right on a way-marked permissive path. Keep on this path in more or less the same direction as it becomes a public path for about ⅔ mile until level with buildings a field away on the right.

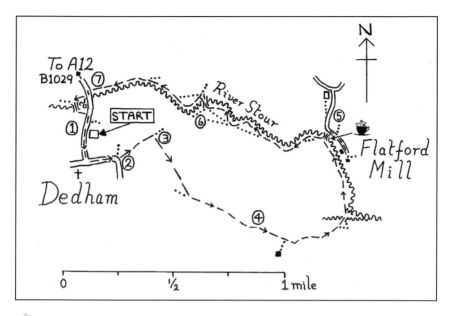

4. Bear half right across the field to a metal kissing gate which gives onto a concrete track leading to the farm. Turn left along the track. When the concrete ends, continue on the unsurfaced track to a kissing gate next to a field gate. Continue on the path in the same direction passing by a concrete sluice and ignoring a path on the right. Continue along the river bank and cross the river to Bridge Cottage and the tea garden.

5. After tea turn right along the lane to see Flatford Mill and Willy Lott's house. Retrace your steps and cross back over the river by the same bridge, then turn right along the river bank, signed 'Dedham'. The right of way lies along the river bank though the actual path lies a little to the left at the time of writing. Watch for a wooden bridge across the river and make for this. Do not go on the path that bears left as this rejoins the outward route.

Flatford Mill was owned by Constable's father. Though John Constable lived mainly in London, his great inspiration was the beautiful countryside in which he spent his happy childhood and to which he often returned. He wrote, 'I love every stile and stump and lane ... as long as I am able to hold a brush, I shall never cease to paint them.' His devotion to these landscapes shines through his paintings. The scenes of many of Constable's famous paintings can still be recognised. Willy Lott's cottage figures in perhaps his best known picture, The Haywain. It was built in about 1600 and is a substantial farmhouse, previously known as Gibbeons Gate Farm, rather than what we might usually think of as a cottage. Willy Lott is said to have lived there for all his 88 years without spending more than four days away.

Flatford Mill and the surrounding buildings were given to the National Trust in 1943. They are leased to the Field Studies Council who use them for a field studies centre. Bridge Cottage, acquired by the National Trust in 1985, now houses a display illustrating Constable's life and work.

Also at Flatford is the RSPB's first wildlife garden. It used to belong to two sisters, Sylvia and Margaret Richardson and they ran a tea garden on the site for decades. They were great nature lovers and they bequeathed their land to the RSPB who have transformed it into a beautiful plot dedicated to demonstrating how we can all encourage wildlife in our gardens. It is open every day in the summer and at weekends in winter. Admission is free and it is well worth taking the time to enjoy, with lots of ideas we can use in our own gardens.

6. Go across the bridge and immediately turn left to continue by the river to a road.

The River Stour was one of the first English rivers to be made passable for barges, early in the 18th century. Flatford was an important centre for this trade and originally had four dry docks for the construction and repair of barges. One, still containing a barge, was found next to Bridge Cottage and excavated in 1988. It is flooded in winter to protect the brickwork. When Constable knew this area, the river would have been alive with barges. The Navigation Company did not own the river bank but paid tolls for the passage of barges to the land owners. These agreements were sometimes on opposite sides of the river, which meant that the towing horses had to be transported across on the barges - a scene shown in Constable's The White Horse. In addition, the horses had to leap more than 120 stiles on the 24 mile journey up river. With such problems it not surprising that water borne traffic rapidly lost out to the railway.

7. Turn left along the road for 30 yards then turn right to continue by the river for about 200 yards. Turn left on a path that leads to a bridge over the river at Dedham Lock. Over the bridge follow the path ahead back to the road and turn right back to the start.

Dedham Mill, to the right of the path, was also owned by the Constable family business and both the lock and mill feature in his pictures. The building we see today is later and has been converted into flats. The lock is also in use as part of the river regulation scheme for the Stour.

Walk 19
LAVENHAM

This walk combines the works of man and nature. It is based round Lavenham, a remarkably well-preserved and attractive wool town that is well worth taking the time to explore. For nigh on 100 years, Lavenham was on the Long Melford to Bury St Edmunds branch line, which opened in August 1865. Lavenham lost its rail service in the 1960s and the track has now become a nature reserve, managed to promote the trees, flowers and birds with a lovely path along it that forms the spine of this walk. The route climbs some 75 feet from the route of the railway to the town. This short ascent is easy and the small effort involved is rewarded with a fine view across the surrounding countryside.

Among the many teashops in Lavenham, it is worth visiting Sweetmeats for its wonderful range of ice creams – I counted 21 in all – made on a Suffolk dairy farm and offered in enterprising combinations. In addition to ice cream and the usual teatime goodies of excellent cakes and cream teas with clotted cream, Sweetmeats offers pancakes with sweet fillings such as amarena cherries with wild cherry and kirsch ice cream. For lunch, doorstep or open sandwiches, ploughmans and filled jacket potatoes are served as well as excellent full meals. The teashop is open every day except Wednesday throughout the year between 10am and 5pm. Telephone: 01787 248442 Website: www.goodfoodarmy.co.uk/sweetmeats

DISTANCE: 4 miles

MAP: OS Explorer 196 Sudbury, Hadleigh and Dedham Vale

STARTING POINT: Lavenham Walk parking area. GR 899490

HOW TO GET THERE: The starting point is on a minor road between Bridge Street on the A134 about two miles north of Long Melford and Lavenham on the A1141. The parking area is where the road crosses a disused railway and lies about half a mile west of Lavenham.

ALTERNATIVE STARTING POINT: If you wish to visit the teashop at the beginning or end of your walk, start in Lavenham where there is ample parking in several car parks. The Cock Inn public car park on the B1071 is well placed. Turn right out of the car park then right again along Water Street to the teashop. You will then start the walk at point 7.

THE WALK

1. From the parking area, take the signed footpath down to a disused railway and turn right. Follow the path until it emerges into a field. Continue along the right hand side of the field with a wood on the right to a track.

2. Turn left along the track and follow it uphill (turn round for the best view of the walk) then continue between farm buildings.

3. Take a track on the left and follow it to a lane.

4. Turn right for about ¼ mile.

5. Turn left on a signed path and follow this across a field and then on between fences to a lane.

As the path leads towards Lavenham the view is dominated by the mighty tower of the church, exactly as intended to demonstrate the wealth and piety of the merchants of the town. The building we see today dates mainly from the end of the 15th century and the beginning of the 16th, so just predates the religious and social

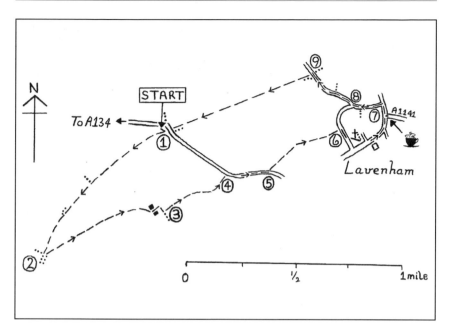

upheavals of the Reformation. It is said that the defeat of Richard III at the Battle of Bosworth in 1485 was the reason the old church was largely torn down and this magnificent edifice constructed. John de Vere, thirteenth Earl of Oxford and lord of the manor of Lavenham was captain-general to the victorious Henry Tudor and de Vere suggested to the prosperous citizens that they build the church together to give thanks to God for the Tudor victory. Seeing how the political wind was blowing, they agreed. Their corporate sponsorship of the church can be seen both on the church tower and the parapet: De Vere's star is prominent upon every face of the tower, whilst Thomas Spring III's coat of arms appear 32 times on the parapet. There are many interesting features but perhaps the most entertaining are the carvings on five misericords. These are shelf like structures in choir stalls used to relieve the requirement to stand through long services and the craftsmen often took the chance to make humorous and rather secular carvings.

6. Turn right for 150 yards and then go up some steps on the left to walk through a churchyard to a road in Lavenham. Turn left and walk through the town to Water Street on the right. Turn right to the teashop a few yards along on the right.

7. Turn left out of the teashop to return to the main road and turn right. Take the first road on the left, Hall Road.

Lavenham is one of the best-preserved medieval towns in England with over 300 buildings listed as being of architectural or historical interest and well worth taking the time to explore. Lady Street more or less opposite the teashop leads up to the square and the famous Guildhall, passing the Tourist Information Centre where a town guidebook is available. Considerable effort has gone into preserving its character, with power and telephone lines being buried and television aerials hidden in lofts. Edwardian neo-Tudor architects set the style of half-timbered buildings being black and white but there has been a return to a more authentic style with the wood frames lime washed a silvery grey and the panels between often painted pink. This is in imitation of the old practice of mixing pigments such as ox blood or sloe juice into the plaster. The massive amounts of timber used in these buildings, far more than is needed for structural stability, is an indication of the wealth of the town in medieval times as mature timber was already scarce and expensive when these houses were built. The wealth was built on wool and the organisation that regulated trade, the Guild of Corpus Christi, built the magnificent Guildhall in Market Place when it received its charter in 1529. This is now in the care of the National Trust and houses a museum (and serves teas!). Behind there is a delightful walled garden with a 19th century mortuary and lockup. The famous Swan Hotel, just across the road from the teashop, was a favourite with American airmen during the Second World War and has a collection of memorabilia and a stretch of bar scored with many of their names.

8. Take the first lane on the right, Park Road, signed as a no through road, as far as a cross path signed 'The Lavenham Walk'.

9. Turn left along this lovely path as far as a bridge. Turn right back to the starting point. (Keep ahead if you started in Lavenham.)

Walk 20
THETFORD FOREST

*E*ssentially this is a woodland walk in Thetford Forest but it has a
fascinating story to tell about man's relationship with Nature in this
infertile corner of Suffolk, a story that reveals itself in the changes in
vegetation along the route. It visits Brandon Country Park, which has a
great tearoom, and the return is an easy stroll along a delightful
woodland path.

☕ Copper Beech Tearoom is named after a fine avenue of trees leading to
the car park. This was one of several avenues, but now is the only one still
standing. It is housed in an attractive and interesting modern building next
to the Visitor Centre with plenty of tables outside among the trees. Open
every day from 10 am until 4.30 pm from March to October and 3pm in
winter, they serve a good choice of sandwiches and cakes as well as very
reasonably priced and tasty main meals. Telephone: 01842 810185. Website:
www.brandoncountrypark.co.uk

DISTANCE: 4 miles
MAP: OS Explorer 229 Thetford Forest in The Brecks
STARTING POINT: Small parking area at Bury Bottom near Brandon GR 792842
HOW TO GET THERE: The parking area is on the east side of the B1106 at a dip in the road a mile south of the entrance to Brandon Country Park and ½ mile north of a track signed to May Day bird hide. At the time of writing it is marked with a number 11 in red on a white background. If this is full, there is a little more space 100 yards south on the west side of the road.
ALTERNATIVE STARTING POINT: If you wish to visit the teashop at the beginning or end of your walk, start in Brandon Country Park where there is ample parking (charge). The teashop is adjacent to the car park. You will then start the walk at point 10.

The walk

The red on white numbers are fire brigade access points in case of fire in the forest so it is important not to block the track.

1. Cross the road and take a narrow path for 150 yards, going over two small cross paths, to join a larger path on a corner by a post topped with orange and purple. Go ahead on this path, soon crossing a wide track. Ignore two tracks on the left to reach a second cross track.

2. Turn left. Ignore a left branch after 60 yards and continue to a major track.

3. Turn right. Ignore a branch right after about 70 yards and all paths to left and right to reach a cross track about 50 yards after a major track joins from the right.

4. Turn right and walk as far as a metal kissing gate into an open fenced area on the right.

Left entirely to nature, this area would be open woodland, but this was cleared about 4,000 years ago by Neolithic farmers. Always a difficult area to farm with thin, infertile soil prone to sand blowing in one of the driest areas of Britain, the main agriculture was traditionally sheep grazing and rabbits farmed in huge warrens. Brandon had two rabbit factories to process the meat and fur. Their grazing promoted the development of heath with a distinctive community of plants and animals. Occasionally, when corn prices were high or the land was sufficiently rested, areas would be broken up and ploughed for a year or two until its fragile

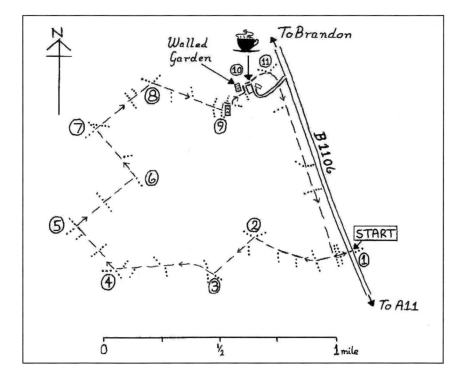

fertility was exhausted again. These 'brecks' gave the area its modern name that came into use in the 1920s.

By the end of the First World War the nation's timber reserves were in a dire state. The government set up the Forestry Commission in 1919, charged with building up a strategic reserve of timber. They bought huge tracts of poor quality farmland and planted them with trees. This included Thetford Forest, the largest lowland forest in the UK. At the time conservation was not seen as important and heathland was regarded as an almost worthless wilderness, to be improved by forestry or intensive agriculture with irrigation and fertilisers. Today we take a different view and appreciate the value of what our forefathers so casually destroyed. The Forestry Commission now leases tracts of land such as this to English Nature to regenerate heath. Grazing is an important part of this process and so the area has to be fenced.

5. Turn right through the gate and follow the path ahead across open heath. Go over the first cross track to a second one.

6. Turn left to a gate out of the heathland enclosure then follow the path ahead for 170 yards to a cross path.

7. Turn right. Go over two cross paths and press on to a third, which can be recognised as it leads between deciduous trees rather than pines and Brandon Park House can be seen at the end.

8. Turn right and keep ahead on this path to arrive at an attractive pond (The Lake) in front of the house.

Edward Bliss bought Brandon Park Estate in the 1820s and he transformed the heath into magnificent parkland, planting an astounding eight million trees in just six months. Brandon was a major centre for gunflint and demand declined at the end of the Napoleonic wars. Many people lost their livelihoods and Bliss employed some of this labour to transform the estate. After planting windbreaks of Scots Pine and European Larch, an arboretum of exotic and unusual species was created. Originally the house had 21 bedrooms, an imposing entrance hall complete with organ, a billiard room and a library as well as a separate laundry, stables for 17 horses, garaging and a generator to provide electric lighting. It is now a nursing home. He also built a Mausoleum, not passed on this route, so he could be buried on his estate.

☕ **9.** Turn left and follow the path as it bends right. A few yards after the end of the pond turn left and follow the path past specimen trees and the Walled Garden to the Visitor Centre and tearoom.

By the end of the First World War the estate had become run down and was incorporated into the new Thetford Forest. The area that is now Brandon Country Park, only a small part of the 2,500 acres Bliss bought, was purchased by Suffolk County Council in 1972. The walled garden was originally the kitchen garden for Brandon House, supplying fruit, vegetables and flowers to the household. It has now been transformed into a most attractive area, lovingly maintained by a team of volunteers.

10. Turn left out of the tearoom and almost immediately turn left again to walk with a play area on the right and very soon bear right way-marked, at the time of writing, by a post topped with red, orange and purple, to a cross track.

11. Turn right. Continue across an entrance drive, guided by an orange and purple topped post. Eventually this delightful path starts to descend gently. At the bottom of the slope turn left back to the start.

(Follow the path round to the right if you started at the teashop.)